SOCCER
AND THE SOUL

Other books by the same author

Sports Psychology in Action
(1995) Oxford, Butterworth Heinemann.

Performance Profiling
(1996) Leeds, NCF Publications.

Sports Psychology in Performance
(1997) Oxford, Butterworth Heinemann.

Golf: A Mind Game
(1999) Cookham, Queensgate Publications (with Peter Galvin).

SOCCER
AND THE SOUL

RICHARD BUTLER

Q

QUEENSGATE PUBLICATIONS

First published in 2000
by Queensgate Publications
Cookham, Berkshire

ISBN 1-902655-05-2

A catalogue record of this book is available from the British Library

Cover design by Charlie Webster
Book design by Production Line, Minster Lovell, Oxford
Production by Landmark Consultants, Princes Risborough,
Buckinghamshire
Printed in England by Cox & Wyman

Contents

Chapter 1

Kick-off

'My life is my work. My work is my life.'
Bill Shankly

Football is a passion. It seeps forever into our soul. 'It is something you can't get out of your system,' suggested Danny Williams as he took the helm at Mansfield Town. Managers and players live the game. Fans, on the other hand, live for the game. Managers and players are steeped in the ethos, although fundamentally their engagement is professional. Soccer, for them, is a living, a means to earn a crust whilst realising ambitions that fans crave to experience.

Players, for the most part, are not fans. Theirs is active participation, an experience often in reality quite mundane. Primarily, the game for them is a job. An occupation, for the most part, saturated with training and recovering from injury. If offered better employment terms at another club, a player will usually move on. The point was made succinctly by Pat Nevin of Kilmarnock when he said, 'Being a footballer is what I do. It isn't what I am.'

For fans the game invades the way they live. Football is their life. 'Football was never meant to have a sense of proportion for fans who care about it,' remarked Clive Tyldesley, as the teams emerged to a glorious fanfare at Wembley for the final international of the millennium between England and Scotland. Fans immerse themselves in the game. They eagerly devour news about the team, scan Teletext for snippets of gossip, traverse the country to watch a match in some windswept town on a cold Tuesday night, re-run videos of momentous goals and blunders, and endlessly chew the fat over an abject performance.

Supporters might be considered to be connoisseurs – enmeshed in a club, tied to the team in an umbilical manner and expert judges of players, managers, team formations and tactics. Unlike players, fans rarely change their allegiances. As John Colquhoun, so aptly a player with Hearts, remarked, 'At birth, God asks you if you want logic or passion. If you want passion then He next allocates you a football team to support.' And you remain loyal. 'Fans are forced to support their team through deep-seated allegiance, geographic or family ties: there is no way out,' suggested Dave Bowler. 'They might wish they didn't support Birmingham City or Luton Town, but they're stuck with it. Scarred for life.'

Membership of a football club is not based on salary, citizenship or old school ties. There are no admission criteria or metaphorical hoops for the prospective member to jump through. The tie is a psychological one. Fans may buy into the club through the purchase of shares, bonds or season tickets, but the only true admission is by way of a psychological bond. Membership results from shared memories, loyalty, aspirations, emotions and sacrifices. Reflecting on last week's dour 0–0 draw and turning out in the rain with a forlorn hope that they just might surprise us this week with a victory against the division leaders is the essence of devotion. The club, in a deep sense, is owned by the committed. Artist Peter Howson captured the fan's love of a team as he described the lasting hold that Ayr United had on him. He said, 'My happiest memories are standing on the terrace with my father, drinking weak Bovril, eating mutton pie, watching Danny McLean running rings round the opposition. It made a perfect Saturday.'

Players, coaches and directors move on. The club and its fans live on. In this sense, Bill Shankly's famous quote – 'Some people think football is a matter of life and death ... I can assure them it is much more serious than that' – expresses something fundamental. Football traverses time. Supporters pass the culture of the club through the generations. Managers, directors and players are, in a sense, gatecrashers. They are entrusted with our club. When they are perceived by the fans to be less than competent or committed, they come in for barracking and demonstrations from the terraces.

The supporter is in it to succour the self. Their engagement both expresses and validates something about themselves. Supporters need soccer to survive. Without it, as the summer break and international weeks demonstrate, fans feel a loss. A part of themselves slides into dormancy. They clamour for involvement, stories, information, and they feverishly tick off the days to the next match.

Supporting a club says something about our self. Glory supporters may align themselves with a successful team, but in doing so they choose success, not a football club. They like it easy, are prepared to bask vicariously in others' glory, live in the slipstream of success and show themselves to be of a type that can readily be bought. 'Shallow' may be another description. As Rick Gekoski suggested in his book on the experience of being a Coventry City supporter, professional soccer may be all about winning, but life isn't. Most of us lose most of the time. He said, 'You can base a life on what you learn watching the Sky Blues. You win occasionally and struggle most of the time.' Supporting the likes of Manchester United breeds unrealistic notions of what life is about. It is a fantasy to believe we win most of the time. The true supporter sticks with his or her team, through the frequent nadirs and rare successes. Supporters may selectively pick the fixture, but the club seems to pick them.

The club is a platform upon which various aspects of ourselves are validated. Our adherence to the team gives meaning to the way we construe or think of ourselves:

- Through our appearance – fans deck themselves in replica shirts and other regalia, the younger ones having their faces splashed abstractly with paint in the team's colours. This is a statement of allegiance and group membership, and also a measure of the individual fan's self-identity. It spells out an act of faith. The message is 'I am a fan of football', but foremost 'I am unswervingly a devout green and white Plymouth Argyle supporter.'
- With our possessions – the young fan's quest for autographs, the purchase of a programme to add to the collection, a David Ginola duvet cover with matching Iain

Dowie pillows to cuddle, hats weighed down with pins and badges, a crested boot bag used as a toiletry bag, those addictive collections of cards and stickers where you amass a dozen Gary Nevilles that no one else would swop spent chewing gum for. One of my personal favourites is an old oak swivel desk chair acquired at an auction of memorabilia on the eve of the destruction of Leeds Road. It was sold as the manager's chair, and on it I envisage the likes of Bill Shankly resting his knurled features and musing over his latest thoughts on the game. As possessions are an extension of ourselves, in the sense that we acquire objects that reflect our needs, so it is that acquiring the club's products gives us a sense of ownership of the club. We buy into the aura of a club. Possessions secure our roots.

- Through our behaviour – the actions we take reveal something about how we see ourselves. We may have pre-match routines or superstitions in the same way that players do. We wear the same moth-eaten flat cap, walk the same route to the ground, buy a dodgy hot dog from the same spotty vendor. Such customs are guilt-evasion acts. They convey a wish to avoid feeling that we are instrumental in our side's poor performance. By implication, they suggest we are connected to our team's performance. Through our actions we may just influence how the match pans out.

- With our verbals – many fans believe their chants of support and calls of derision influence the way the team and individuals perform. The way we express ourselves is a reflection of how we are. The centre-forward fluffs a gilt-edged chance. Whether we react with 'poor show old chap', 'you stupid effing load of pig's tripe' or 'I guess he was caught off balance' tells something about the type of person we are.

- Through the athletic side to ourselves – as supporters our involvement is vicarious. We like to think we would have tucked away the penalty or crossed the ball on to the striker's head rather than ballooning it into the stand. Our anticipated success corroborates the view we have of ourselves as being the undiscovered George Best or Dino Zoff.

- Through the academic in us – our appetite for understanding and knowledge makes us a student of the game. But we learn through observation, not through participation. Rick Gekoski made this point with a perceptive analysis of how players react to punters' views. He noted, 'While the pros are polite to supporters, they think them fools. Not because they always have the wrong opinions, but because they hold them without having earned the right to them. Because they don't know what it is like, haven't served their time.'

- Morally – our moral and ethical dimension is served through engagement with football. Rules of play establish what is permissible and what is forbidden. A certain discipline is expected of players both in reference to the rules and in keeping to the manager's game plan. How often do we see a player being rollocked from the sidelines, or even substituted for not sticking to his role? 'Let us not forget that the place of truth for an athlete is, and always will be, the stadium,' mused the French poet Eric Cantona. And fans would agree. They go to see their idols perform, to excel, to reach their peak week in, week out. Match days may take on an almost religious status, with the modern stadium akin to the church that we attend to worship the team and pray for success or the final whistle when we are hanging on to a slender lead. Some fans' devotion is so strong that they request that, after their own demise, their ashes be scattered on to the pitch. Some clubs now place restrictions on or deny the fan this last request. Rangers, through their manager, John Greig, explained their ban on ashes being cast on to the Ibrox pitch by reasoning 'we were doing so many that we were ending up with big bald patches, even in the middle of summer'.

- Through esteem – good performances lift supporters. They sing about their abiding faith to the club and raise their clenched fists to the heavens when the goals go in. David Pleat aptly said that 'Winning isn't the end of the world.' Perhaps not, but winning does give supporters a surge of pride. To walk home after the game with dignity and self-respect; to go into work next day with a glow of contentment; to know, for another few days at least, they are protected from the baiting and ribbing of other supporters.

A central aim of this book revolves around developing an understanding of the game through applying a psychological framework. I am a clinical and sports psychologist, have a passion for soccer and am a lifelong supporter of Huddersfield Town. I look for other results, particularly for those of Rochdale, Hartlepool United, Blackburn Rovers, Halifax Town, Doncaster Rovers, West Bromwich Albion and Third Lanark (before it ceased to exist). I notice these are mostly northern industrial towns and they are all sides that tend to struggle season upon season. This, of course, says volumes about me. Not least that I like to grapple with the less glamorous. I have also recently developed a fondness for Forfar Athletic after discovering their nickname to be the 'Loonies'. This of course says something else about me.

In exploring the psychology of soccer, I have endeavoured to be guided by four principles:

1. A focus on the experience of the participants. Footballers make their living from playing. They communicate their skills visually in the patterns they create on the pitch, not verbally. During interviews, players rarely provide an insight into their thinking, generally relying on bland cliché and rhetoric designed to keep the voracious press at bay. As Tony Adams once said, 'I'm a professional footballer, not a man of words.' However, throughout the book I have sought to illustrate points with quotes from players, coaches and managers. Sometimes there are real gems, which exactly encapsulate a meaning. There are also some wonderful quotes, full of cluttered metaphors, such as Glenn Hoddle's comment 'That chance came to him on a plate out of the blue', which nevertheless communicates a meaning understood by most supporters.

2. Identification of aspects that are considered to be important for a top-class player. Inevitably, there are myriad views as to what attributes are important. Terry Venables described how he arrived

at his viewpoint: 'We actually got a formula down on paper. It comes in four parts: technical, tactical, personality [mental strength] and pace. These headings, I think, cover all the ingredients required to make a good player, and you give marks out of ten for each section.' In this way a player's overall ability could theoretically be measured.

Ajax, in Holland, similarly have four central tenets and base coaching around the development of these qualities. The acronym the club uses is PITS, standing for personality, intelligence, technique and speed. Interestingly, what can be deduced from El Tel's omission of intelligence? Without becoming enmeshed in the debate about the necessary make-up of a top player, I have sought to provide, through each chapter, an outline of all the attributes that might be considered necessary. A sports psychologist might encourage players and coaches to rate themselves on such qualities, in order to provide an estimate of strengths and weaknesses in what is known as a Performance Profile (Butler 1999). The interested reader might mischievously wish to rate some of their team's players on each quality, to build up a profile and monitor their progress through the season.

3. Football is a way of life. Alan Ball senior taught his son this. He said, 'I taught football to him, not as a game, but as a way of life.' All the attributes that make a player what he is, are attributes that are necessary to excel in life outside football. They are, in effect, life skills. This is often, within sports psychology, considered a truism. If players demonstrate confidence, teamwork, emotional control, leadership, ability to handle pressure and so forth on the pitch, they should in theory be well equipped to employ these successfully in life off the pitch. However, many footballers' lives go astray. The book seeks to pick up some of the contrasts between what might be expected and what does happen. Retirement from the game is one example of a time when footballing skills might be expected to transfer to the outside world.

However, even with a World Cup winner's medal, life outside playing football does not come easy. Consider what the 1966 World Cup winning team were doing 30 years on from the great day. Gordon Banks was self-employed in sports promotion after finishing football prematurely following a car accident; George Cohen had won a five-year battle with cancer and developed interests in property development; Ray Wilson was an undertaker; Nobby Stiles was co-ordinator of Manchester United's school of excellence; Jack Charlton had been a manager of some note at Middlesbrough, Newcastle United, Sheffield Wednesday and the Republic of Ireland; Bobby Moore had briefly managed Southend and tragically died of cancer on 24 February 1993, aged 51; Alan Ball had remained in football, coaching and managing Blackpool, Bristol Rovers, Portsmouth, Stoke City, Exeter City, Southampton and Manchester City; Roger Hunt was a member of the Pools Panel and ran his own haulage business; Geoff Hurst had managed Chelsea briefly and moved on to manage a company selling car warranties; Bobby Charlton was briefly player manager at Preston North End and had become a director at Manchester United; and Martin Peters had been player-manager at Sheffield United before working alongside Geoff Hurst in the same motor insurance company.

4. Football is a microcosm of life. The knocks, the disappointments, the joy of success, the short straw of being drawn away at Arsenal in the FA Cup. Football distributes emotional contrasts. How players react tells us something about them – in life as in football. The actions and performances on the field of play express the way they are. Body language informs us about a player's confidence. His expression tells us about his mood. The way a player moves, his style, gives a glimpse of the player's psychological structure.

Some players appear to play the game as they play their lives. They apply the same psychological structures to both. Bobby Moore was a prime example: 'The measure and perfectionism of his football was mirrored in his everyday life,' noted Jeff Powell. Kenny Dalglish was a perfectionist, disciplined, determined, competitive on the pitch and off. The pitch is an extension of how he is in real life. These same attributes are probably also those he applied to management, and they are also particularly suited to that role - hence his success. However, a perfectionist streak may create vulnerability for a manager. Perfection is difficult to achieve when we are dependent on others to reach the goals we set. Was this the reason for the stress and pressure that pushed Kenny to resign at both Liverpool and Blackburn Rovers? Some players, perhaps those with a flamboyant approach, use the pitch to express themselves - they display confidence, take risks, are a law unto themselves. But these, it might be argued, are not the attributes of a good manager, and this may explain why mavericks generally fail to be effective managers.

Other players have two selves: they elaborate aspects of themselves on the pitch, but outside football they are very different – they have another personality. Vinnie Jones at home is caring and protective – hardly a template to succeed on a wet Saturday afternoon away at Barnsley. A second persona, for the pitch, shows a different side of Vinnie. Tony Currie was quiet, thoughtful and an introvert off the pitch, but on it he blossomed into an artist, dominating the field of play. Such players have selves that can be presented to the public and a different self that dominates away from the glare of the floodlights.

Yet other players are seemingly caught in a neurotic paradox. They act in ways that are self-defeating. They bring their everyday self on to the pitch with disastrous consequences. They have ways of being that do not transfer well on to the pitch. The cool, arrogant, petulant characteristics of playboy-dom may be successful in the night-club, but they serve only to bring trouble when expressed on the football pitch. The division between the two selves – the footballing self and the private self – is often expressed by players wishing to keep their private life from the media, but when they act as playboys on the pitch they suffer the scrutiny of both selves.

Kevin Keegan stated that 'A hell of a lot of football is about psychology. The six inches between a player's ears can be the most important part of his body.' This book seeks to open a window into the world of soccer and to provide the supporter with a psychological understanding of the game we treasure.

Chapter 2

The gifted

'Gods against boys.'
Ron Atkinson

Competence can be simply defined as having the ability to perform. At the very least, a player must be able to do the job that is asked of him. Players are often described as dependable, professional or even businesslike, and it is difficult to believe players could reach the professional ranks without being reasonably proficient, without consistently giving a good account of themselves.

However, there are numerous perspectives that can be employed in analysing a player's capabilities, or lack of them. Many players 'slip through the net' at one club, only to prove their worth elsewhere and then maddeningly, but perhaps inevitably, come back to haunt the club that turned them away.

Players assess themselves, as it were, from the inside. They know their strengths and weaknesses. They play the game that makes sense to them. If a player construes himself as a grafter, he'll play in ways that validate this notion. He'll run for lost causes, work his bollocks off in midfield and close people down throughout the 90 minutes. Football is an act of self-expression. A player displays something of himself, his style of play and his assessment of his own competence each time he sets foot on the pitch. Some players are more eloquent on the pitch than off it. For example, Mark Hughes said, 'When I get on the field I've always found that I can express myself better than I can off it.'

Everyone else – coach, manager, other players, supporters, pundits and critics – makes assessments from the 'outside'. They look on and judge a player according to their own values. Some players are perceived to exceed expectations and become stars. They

consistently excite and amaze the onlookers with their skills.
Creativity is often at the core of their class. They try new ideas, take
calculated risks, and are not afraid of trying out new things on the
world stage. Rob Steen, in waxing eloquently about those who seek
to excite through invention and a broadening of their horizons, said,
'Irreverence and daring are their bywords; safe options, anathema.'

Greatness or genius is the zenith. It is reserved for a very few.
The accolade of greatness might be considered where players:

- 'Have great games in great games.' (Sir Matt Busby)
- 'Do things that are different, things the ordinary player
  cannot do.' (Sir Matt Busby again)
- Create time through nanosecond ball control.
- Dictate the game under pressure.
- Have teams built around them. We would perhaps hardly
  consider Brian Clough's teams to have been constructed
  around stars, yet Clough revealed something about the
  esteem he held for his left-winger, John Robertson, in a
  question he put to Martin O'Neill: 'What's the point of
  giving you the ball when there's a genius on the other wing?'
- Create opportunities for others and themselves; as Bob
  Paisley suggested, they 'are normally like soloists in an
  orchestra'.
- Do the unexpected. Sir Matt Busby said, 'Great players are
  individualists. That's what makes them great players. They
  do not conform readily. They do the unexpected. That is
  also why they are great players. If they did what was
  expected they would be ordinary players.' Tony
  Waddington, who managed the likes of Alan Hudson and
  Tony Currie at Stoke City, made the point that, with a great
  player, coaching is almost redundant. He said, 'I don't tell
  thoroughbreds how to play. It is the unexpected that excites
  people, and players, not coaches, provide that.' John
  Motson also had a hazy thought about the unexpected
  when he described Tino Asprilla as 'totally unpredictable,
  but perfectly capable of doing the unexpected'.
- Are essentially 'good eggs'. Gordon Strachan suggested that
  'the greatest players in the world are all good men. I don't

think they really cause you a problem. The ones who've got a problem are those who think they're top players.'

According to a survey in *Four Four Two* Magazine, the ten greatest players of all time were:

1. Pelé

111 caps, 97 goals

Known as Dico to his family, Pelé scored on his debut for Santos at 15 years of age. He was 17 when he scored twice in the 1958 World Cup final. Pelé described the more memorable of his two goals thus: 'Nilton Santos kicked a long ball ... I stopped it on my thigh, kicked it in the air, whirled and kicked it towards the goal as it came down.' He is the only man in history to have won three World Cup winners medals.

Pelé was widely acknowledged as a genius. 'He had everything. Two good feet. Magic in the air. Quick. Powerful. Could beat people with skill. Could outrun people. Only 5'8" tall yet he seemed a giant of an athlete on the pitch. Perfect balance and impossible vision,' said Bobby Moore. He had balance, fantastic ball control, vision (as evidenced by his famous attempt to beat the Czech goalkeeper from the half-way line), power in both legs and body, an ability to hang in the air (as he did in scoring his goal against Italy in the 1970 World Cup final), guile, anticipation, and the mental strength not to retaliate under severe provocation. *Four Four Two* enlarged further: 'He leaps like a long jumper, sprints better than most 100 metre runners, and he could trap the ball in mid-air.'

Pelé first suggested that football is 'the beautiful game'. He elaborated further: 'The full beauty of the game is best seen in the inventiveness, the ingenuity, and the skill of the players both individually and in team combination, and this is only seen in an attacking style of football.'

Pelé unfortunately never graced the famed Wembley turf. His only appearance in London was in 1972, playing for Santos against Fulham in a friendly at Craven Cottage. He scored a penalty, but was on the losing side as Fulham won 2–1.

2. Johan Cruyff

48 caps, 33 goals

Three times winner of the European Footballer of the Year award, Cruyff had vision, a presence that inspired team-mates, self-belief, a remarkable ability to create space and an uncanny knack of reading the game. Ruud Gullit suggested, 'He knew everything about the game. He was a perfectionist.' If Pelé appealed to our aesthetic side, Cruyff was the thinking man's vision. *Four Four Two* added that 'He terrified outclassed opponents with his masterly presence ... He had a wide repertoire of skills and the versatility to torment any opposition.'

3. George Best

37 caps, 9 goals

George was never able to pitch his skills on the world stage, which many, including Rodney Marsh, regret. Marsh said, 'If George had played in the World Cup he would have been the greatest player of all time.' Best had balance, pace, tremendous ball control, the knack of spotting his opponents' weaknesses, wonderful ability to beat his man and coolness under pressure. Jimmy Greaves said, 'George Best was the greatest player of my time when it came to flair and mind-boggling invention.' Danny Blanchflower, his Northern Ireland compatriot, suggested, 'Basically, Best makes a greater appeal to the senses than Stanley Matthews or Tom Finney. His movements are quicker, lighter, more balletic ... he has ice in his veins, warmth in his heart, timing and balance in his feet.'

4. Diego Maradona

90 caps, 34 goals

Maradona had masterful dribbling and ball control, yet he was sulky, petulant and egotistical, with a tendency to intimidate referees and supporters. Few who saw his behaviour in the 1990 World Cup final will forget his barrel-chested dodgem-like retaliation to most refereeing decisions. He had a tendency to mark most occasions with controversy. 'He has wonderful control but handles the ball and himself badly,' said *Four Four Two*, taking a sideswipe at the two sides of his character. Maradona retired and came back many times because, as he said, 'There's a little bug telling me you still can.'

5. Franz Beckenbauer

103 caps, 14 goals
Cool, with immaculate reading of the game, Beckenbauer was largely responsible for the genesis of the sweeper role. He read the game from the back, moved gracefully with the ball and was able to make the telling pass with uncanny accuracy. Many sweepers have sought to model Beckenbauer's poise and measured approach, but he remains the master.

6. Alfredo di Stefano

31 caps (for Argentina and Spain), 26 goals
'He had the talent to beat players by himself, but preferred to wait for team-mates to find space off the ball and receive a perfectly placed pass,' summarised *Four Four Two*.

7. Michel Platini

72 caps, 42 goals
Also three times winner of the European Footballer of the Year award, Platini was the pivot and main influence on a world-class French midfield. As *Four Four Two* noted, 'His vision was breath-taking, his composure elegant, his perception rare.'

8. Kenny Dalglish

102 caps, 30 goals
'That wee fat boy won't make a footballer,' said Alex Ferguson on playing against Kenny in an Old Firm reserve match. He was later

made to eat his words for Dalglish became a great. According to Lou Macari, a team-mate with him in the Celtic reserves, Dalglish was 'a genius, but he became a genius through hard graft'. Dalglish was calm, calculating and competitive. He influenced games with his neat sharp passing and ability to hold and shield the ball with his back to goal, allowing team-mates time and space to run off him. Bob Paisley remarked that, 'When Kenny shines, the whole team shines.' As Dalglish was nothing if not consistent, this meant Liverpool were rarely not on song. Tommy Smith said, 'He was the best player I ever lined up with … his talent was heaven sent' and George Best believed Dalglish was 'on a par with di Stefano'. *Four Four Two* suggests that 'Dalglish allied ball skills that would have had a Brazilian turning Liverpool-red with pride to a determination and grit that left even Graeme Souness feeling soft.'

Dalglish had two good feet, an ability to ride tackles and a voracious appetite for the game. He understood space, and his quick thinking and incisive passing and running set up many goal attempts for colleagues. His passes inside the full back were devastating. His balance was aided by arms that 'splayed out like a bird,' as Sean Fallon, his coach at Celtic, noted. 'Kenny played every game as if it were his last,' said Bobby Lennox of Celtic. David O'Leary provides a defender's perspective: 'You never seem to get a free header against him because he's so good at backing into you. Trying to get the ball off him is almost impossible. He crouches over the ball, legs spread and elbows poking out and defies you to try and get it off him.'

9. Bobby Charlton

106 caps, 48 goals

Charlton was known for his grace, his almost ambassadorial presence on the pitch, and the timing and power of his shooting. *Four Four Two* notes that, 'He didn't beat a player by pace or pure ball control. He just kicked the ball in front of him and ran after it. His swerve did the rest.'

10. Bobby Moore

108 caps, 2 goals

Pelé said of Moore: 'He is he greatest defender I have ever faced.' Ron Greenwood said, 'Bobby was one of the few truly great players who could make the game look simple.' Moore was a leader of men: 'A cool calculating footballer I could trust with my life,' said Sir Alf Ramsey. Sir Alf also noted that he was 'My general on the field who translates our strategy into reality.'

Booby Moore was composed, seemingly unaffected by pressure, had perfected the timing of tackles and read the game with amazing anticipation. As Jock Stein said, 'He knows what's happening 20 minutes before anybody else.'

Bobby Moore tragically died on 24 February 1993. His friend, the reporter Jeff Powell, gave a tribute that extends far beyond Bobby's influence on the field when he said, 'Bobby had the style, the charm and the intelligence to walk with kings … He was the representative supreme of the working man's game, becoming the symbol of hope to so many … He was majestic, living proof that we could all make good … Bobby was the sixties' icon. His was the decade in which the trapdoor of opportunity opened so that talent, irrespective of background, could come thrusting into the light.'

'It is one of the game's unwritten laws that players always seem better when people look back on them,' said Kenny Dalglish, as this top 10 readily illustrates. Other all-time great players, current and past masters, include:

Ruud Gullit

World and European Footballer of the Year in 1987, Ruud was the youngest Dutch professional ever, making his debut at 16 at centre-half for Haarlem in the first division. This was an early illustration of his versatility, as Gullit was able to play any position from sweeper to striker with equal tactical awareness. Mark Hughes said, 'Gullit is genuinely world class, a player you can put anywhere in the side and he plays with presence and stature.'

Glenn Hoddle, who would later sign Ruud for Chelsea, said,

'Gullit shows the difference there is between a good player and a great one. He influences the whole team. He can make simple passes and really dictate the play, making others perform to the best of their ability, even when he's not at his own peak.' Harry Harris made a similar point when Ruud played for the wonderful Milan side that swept Europe before them. He said, 'Gullit was the key factor in the team, the man who could motivate other players and bring the best out of his team mates.' Gullit took command of games. As Glenn Hoddle astutely observed, watching 'Ruud Gullit was like watching a 18 year old playing a game for 12 year olds.'

Ruud was elegant, playing, as Harry Harris noted, 'as if there was no pressure at all, while others would tremble. A big match player, he thrived on the pressure. He stood tall, his presence dominating the pitch.' 'He has time on the ball even when he is being pressurised,' noted Glenn Hoddle. Kees Rijvers, the Dutch manager, said, 'Gullit has no fear, he is stronger than any other player, his pace is electrifying and the power of his shots frightens goalkeepers.'

Gullit's range of passing, vision and ability on the ball were a trademark: 'A player who can win a game with one pass,' remarked Glenn Hoddle. He was also pretty classy in the air. His devastating ball skills led to Alan Hansen remarking, 'It was like watching Hoddle with pace.'

Gullit was not easily dispossessed. Mark Hughes, himself an expert on shielding the ball, noted that, 'He is very difficult to shake off the ball because he is such a big man and he has pace, strength and a natural footballing ability.' Gullit himself put it like this: 'If you keep possession of the ball, you can dictate the game, and wait for the right moment to attack.' Gullit is sincere, modest and charming, with boundless belief in his own ability. His performances oozed class and composure, yet he unassumingly said, 'You never know what to expect, all I can do is express myself at my best.'

Frank Worthington

'The working man's George Best,' announced his manager, Ian Greaves, for whom Frank won honours with both Huddersfield Town and Bolton Wanderers. Worthington had style and faultless ball control, and was lethal and powerful with both feet. 'He was the finest player I'd ever seen in his position,' said compatriot Mike Summerbee.

'I was told that whenever I received the ball I should try and do something special,' Frank was to say. Off the pitch he was equally forthcoming. He said, 'I've always been a bit of a peacock, but that was just me doing my own thing. I used to get a lot of stick for the way I dressed but that was my identity. It didn't really matter whether people accepted me or not.'

Tony Currie

Currie was languid and graceful, and he possessed uncanny ball control. Ken Furphy, his manager, saw his greatness: 'Pelé and Tony were very similar. Pelé couldn't keep the ball as long with people snapping at his heels.' 'Tony had strength, vision and awareness, two good feet and a penchant for the spectacular, whether in the guise of a 40 yard cross-field pass or a long range drive,' noted Rob Steen, and later added: 'Tony Currie was not merely the most complete but also the most compelling English midfield co-ordinator of the seventies.' Tom Finney remarked, 'Although he does the bulk of his work in midfield, he can still come through on the break to score, and score well.'

Currie was a perfectionist. Anything less than a superb performance annoyed him. He said, 'I want to be a perfectionist. I'm disgusted with myself if I give a bad ball. I feel I've failed.' His team-mates also saw this in him. Trevor Hockey, at Sheffield United, said, 'If he hit a bad pass he'd go off his game for a quarter of an hour. You had to kid him through a match.'

Tony was a dilemma in many respects. Never honoured as he perhaps should have been, he often languished in teams that depended heavily on his artistry. Stan Bowles, for one, was perplexed by Currie: 'He'd never speak in training, never really have a laugh ... he was a completely different person on the field, a bit of a strange fish. I don't think he realised how good he was.' Tony himself had this to say: 'I wasn't lazy or an individual. I was a team player who blew kisses to the crowd.'

Glenn Hoddle

'The best passer of the ball in the world,' remarked Don Howe. *Four Four Two* summarised Glenn's ability: 'Balance, control, vision and power, and his ability to hit millimetre-perfect long passes and curling free kicks was nothing short of breathtaking.'

Marco van Basten

Three times European Footballer of the Year, van Basten's career was ended prematurely through injury. His speed of thought was legendary. In line with many of the top Dutch players, he was regarded as complete: 'He's got everything: quick, strong, good in the air, powerful in his shooting from long range or short range, and yet creative,' said Gary Lineker. Ruud Gullit suggested that 'Nothing in the world can put him off. He has incredible mental strength. No matter how much people criticise him, he just does not get worked up,' Gullit later added, 'He could do things on one square yard of grass, which other players can't even dream of.'

Duncan Edwards

Duncan made his England debut at 18 years old and he was described by the United Alphabet as 'Wonderful in the air and a stunning exponent of the cross-field pass ... his bold buccaneering upfield sorties and fierce accurate shooting with either foot caused havoc in the best of defences ... He had the ideal temperament to cope with the special gift of genius.' A victim of the Munich air crash in February 1958, Duncan died in his sleep, aged only 21, after battling for his life for three weeks. Two stained glass windows are dedicated to his memory at St Francis Church in his home town of Dudley.

Gianfranco Zola

Brian Glanville described Zola as 'a possessed imp, wonderfully elusive, technically superb, surprisingly strong and a magician of the dead ball kick'. He concluded that 'Genuine class is permanent and Zola possesses it in spades.'

Alan Hudson

Alan had his admirers on the field as well as off it. *Four Four Two* magazine suggested he was 'The greatest midfield player England never really had.' Peter Osgood, with whom he played at Chelsea, suggested, 'Alan Hudson was one of the greatest players I have ever played with or even saw. Even at 17 he had incredible skills, great brain, great stamina. The only thing he couldn't do was score goals.' Another team-mate at Chelsea, David Webb, remarked, 'When he got the ball he'd create something, work out how he was going to get the ball back to where we needed it.' When Hudson moved to Stoke City, manager Tony Waddington gave him a green bib on his first practice match and reportedly instructed the rest of the assembled squad, 'Whenever you get the ball, just give it to the green bib.'

Michael Owen

Michael is the youngest player to score for England and the country's acknowledged hero of the 1998 World Cup. Kevin Keegan applauded his contribution: 'Michael Owen has made as big an impact on world football as Cruyff, Maradona and Pelé.' He came of age and, when still only 18, his manager at Liverpool, Roy Evans, said, 'You can't talk about potential with Michael any more. He's there already, the full player.'

Emmanuel Petit

League champion, FA Cup winner, World Cup winner and Charity Shield winner in one season, his first at Arsenal, Petit was central to the transformation of Arsenal into an attractive and dangerous side. Petit dictates the play with his work rate, ball winning, vision and immaculate distribution.

Charlie George

Charlie was the inspiration of the Arsenal side of the early 1970s. Frank McLintock, his captain, said he had, 'Tremendous vision, tremendous shot ... some of the things he did in training reminded me of Best.' Charlie, not noted for his modesty, said, 'I always knew I could play. I didn't need anyone to tell me.' He went on, 'I was very self-assured, even when I was a young kid. I did what I thought was right.' Charlie's temperament was sometimes considered a little suspect and his motivation was not always focused where his manager hoped it would be. For example, he once reflected, 'I was arrogant. I used to take the piss out of people, make mugs out of them.' George Graham, his partner up front for Arsenal, both acclaimed his skill and criticised his contribution in one swift sentence, saying, 'He could do the unpredictable ... but he never got involved enough in a game.'

Others who have graced the green and would surface in a Hall of Fame include:

Paul Gascoigne, for his passion, infectious enthusiasm, direct dribbling, subtle probing of defences, and unfortunately his acts of showmanship off and on the pitch. Actor Michael Caine said of Paul, 'He reminds me of Marilyn Monroe. She wasn't the greatest actress in the world, but she was a star so you didn't mind if she was late.'

Gheorghe Hagi, whose subtlety and ball control were unsurpassed, and of whom Johan Cruyff said, 'If you give him time he'll either kill you off himself or use his imagination to create something for a team-mate.'

Chris Waddle, of languid disposition, who persistently teased defenders with feints and shimmying. He once remarked that, 'Football is about kissing the ball, not smacking it about.'

Denilson, who has exceptional ball control and the ability to fool defenders with his balance and feints. He said, 'This business of me holding on to the ball too long doesn't bother me. I have my own style of play and whether people praise or criticise it is not my problem.'

Alan Shearer, noted for his strength on the ball, being difficult to dispossess, his determined approach in every game and the ruthless quality of his finishing.

David Ginola: 'He has pace, trickery and vision. You
are not supposed to have all three,' said Kevin Keegan.

Eusebio: 'He tormented defenders with his devastating
acceleration, fluid technique and ferocious shooting
power,' commented *Four Four Two*.

Puskas, scorer of 83 goals for Hungary, apparently used
to amuse colleagues by juggling a bar of soap in the air
with his famous left foot.

Kevin Beattie, who was unequalled in being able to read
the game from the back, tackled like a sledgehammer and
dominated others in the air.

Anders Limpar, who was, according to Joe Royle, 'a genius
in terms of sheer ability'.

Paul McGrath, who, according to an astute banner at the
Baseball Ground, 'limps on water'.

Rio Ferdinand: 'He was outstanding. For a 19 year old he's
so good it's frightening. You have to build a team around
people like him,' said his manager, Harry Redknapp.

Matthew Le Tissier, scorer of wonderful goals, of whom
his manager at Southampton, Dave Jones, said, 'The
important thing is to get the ball to him in dangerous
areas and then there is nobody better to exploit it.'

Peter Beardsley, whom Dave Hill suggested, 'has an ability
to find and exploit space in and around the penalty area;
superb ball control; an unselfish capacity to create and
the imagination to recognise creative possibilities'.

Gareth Barry, of whom his Aston Villa team-mate Paul
Merson said, 'He has so much ability it just makes me
laugh.'

Bryan Robson, who, according to Ron Atkinson, 'is the
finest, the greatest, the most rounded and accomplished
footballer I have ever been blessed to work with'.

Zinedine Zidane, who Brian Moore reckoned has 'the
body of a bear, the mind of a fox, and ... er ... terrific skill'.

Alan Hansen, of whom team-mate David Johnson said,
'He gave the impression that he could play with a gin
and tonic in one hand and a book in the other.'

And finally:

Ronaldo, who, when compiling his own list of great players, suggested, 'I'm not really Jesus Christ. I'm lower down the line.'

Chapter 3

Not so gifted

'He had it all. The only thing he lacked was ability.'
Tommy Docherty

Tommy Docherty's uncharitable summary of Tony Hateley is a damning assessment of one professional by another. It is rare for a player to be singled out in such a way. More usually the manager will slam the whole team in a collective swipe at a poor performance. Barry Fry aptly remarked, 'We are not a bad side. We create plenty of chances. The trouble is, we keep missing them.' Perhaps the only occasions on which a manager feels free to criticise particular players are when they inherit them, when they feel publicly let down by them or when they leave the club.

Dave Bassett took charge of a wayward Dutch striker when he became manager at Nottingham Forest, and claimed, somewhat tongue in cheek, after one of his better performances, 'I thought Pierre [van Hooijdonk] did very well against Doncaster. He showed what a class player he really is.' John Gregory finally lost patience with Stan Collymore at Aston Villa when the striker's emotional status impeded his commitment to training. Roy Hodgson blamed his dismissal from Blackburn Rovers on Tim Sherwood, his captain, for failing to fully back his plans. Brian Clough, that shy wallflower, summed up Gary McAllister's ability with 'You can't head the ball, you can't tackle and you can't chase back,' as he sought to sign him from Leicester City. Needless to say, the deal fell through. Bob Gansler, USA coach, on resigning from his post, hammered the whole team by saying, 'I can't teach lame ducks to fly any more.'

Players rarely criticise each other, yet Victor Kasule was heard to say of his Shrewsbury Town team-mate, Steve Pittman, 'I thought

I was bad but compared to me, he was the devil incarnate.'
Supporters are of course in a far better position to express their
opinion. They will openly vent their feelings at matches and
publicly denounce whoever they see fit in bars, workplaces and
sometimes in the media. They criticise those in the team, in
contrast to managers, who tend to criticise those not in the team. It
is difficult for the fan to assimilate the reasons why high-profile
transfers turn into low-ability players when they run out in your
team colours, why the bright prospect fades into obscurity or why
players' careers spiral downwards the moment they sign for your
club. The worrying excuse of 'taking time to settle' can be a convenient euphemism for 'useless over-rated waste of space'.

'According to legend, Eskimos have over a hundred words to
describe snow. Significantly the Scots have more than a hundred
words to describe someone who's crap at football,' stated Stuart
Cosgrove. Fans are masterfully adept at judging a player's capabilities. They readily know which players can't pass water, can't beat
an egg, or can't hit a cow's arse with a banjo. They recognise those
who ooze a lack of talent, have the pace of a dead rat, the work
rate of a park bench and the presence of a pile of camel dung. They
know those goalkeepers who have chocolate wrists or who deal
with a cross like a drunk man chasing a balloon. It does not take
such a perceptive eye to notice that the player who leathers the ball
into the stand when he has time to trap it and make a cup of tea is
perhaps as useful as a jelly trumpet.

A most tragic scenario is the one in which, with a blinding flash
of light, a player comes to realise he is perhaps not as remarkable
as he thought. This is exemplified in David James's comment: 'It's
tough when you go to your local supermarket and the person at
the checkout is thinking "dodgy keeper"!'

The perennial dilemma for the fan relates to the continued selection of players who are widely regarded as some way short of the
mark. How do they still make the team? They are perhaps not the
first name on the team-sheet, but they are nevertheless regular
performers, strutting their ill-coordinated stuff in your team
colours. If players are that bad, how can they ever have bypassed
the tuned eyes of scouts and coaches to reach the first team? In
some cases, they even achieve international honours. Alan Fraser,

writer for the *Daily Mail*, posed a similar question in an article with the headline: 'Shy, short sighted, unable to handle the back pass rule ... and accident prone. So how DID Jim Leighton become a World Cup legend?'

There are the good players who fail to hack it at a higher level. There are the good players who fail to fit in with the team's style of play (which of course is a slight to the judgement of the manager who purchased them). There are also good players seeing out lucrative contracts at lesser clubs in the wake of the Bosman ruling who couldn't give a toss week in and week out.

Some teams carry players. Good teams can possibly afford to hide one incompetent in their ranks. The great Brazilian teams had suspect goalkeepers; teams employing long-ball tactics do not rely on midfield maestros; poor full backs are covered by excellent sweepers; or statuesque central defenders are protected by ball-winning midfield players.

There are also more complex reasons why useless players continue to be picked. Some, on the manager's say-so, do a specific job effectively. A player might cross a ball with the artistry of an epileptic clown or be unable to control the ball with any part of his anatomy, but if he can tackle and harass in midfield like a deranged bull terrier, he's the man for the job. What remains a footballing mystery, however, is why such players fail to improve their other skills. Is practice in crossing and ball control denied or not thought worthwhile?

There is also the 'halo effect'. This rests on the manager having seen something of note in the player, and then tending to broaden his positive view in assuming that all aspects of his play are good. Bad passes, mistimed tackles and fluffed chances are overlooked or excused as 'unlike him'. For the fan there is the flipside – the 'donkey effect' – which may apply to the same player, usually construed as over-rated. Here a view is formed of how bad a player is, and all the errors the player makes simply reaffirm the fan's view of him as being completely useless.

A further explanation, with managers fearing they might be viewed as dropping a ripe one, is that they play such players to justify their belief. Managers feel unable to criticise those whom they have purchased and thrown good money at in terms of a long contract, and who quickly prove to be talentless clumsy oafs. If you have shelled out millions, you play them regardless. So, paradoxically, managers may feel compelled to continue playing their signings, hoping something works to validate the buy and prove themselves right. They continue to select the useless. Andy Cole, a major Manchester United signing, said, 'I'd love to know why people look at me and perceive me as a bad player. If you knew why, you'd try and sort out the problem.' He seems to be suggesting that, even within the club, there is resistance to improving players in whom vast amounts of money have been invested. It is as though the transfer fee defines the quality. To then ask a player to improve on some aspect of his game challenges the manager's judgement in buying him.

Managers tend to frame players in terms of performances. Players find themselves variously described as slipshod, toothless, useless, sloppy, having gone missing or lost their touch, not convincing, a liability or having a nightmare. A bad performance does not, by itself, make a bad player. And, like fans, managers will grudgingly accept a poor performance, if they perceive the player is giving of his best. Here are a few musings by managers and commentators over inept performances:

'If my footballers were bricklayers the house they built would fall down.' (Alan Ball as Portsmouth crash 3–0 at Ipswich)

'The back four of the Marie Celeste.' (Alan Hansen)

'We've played quite naively – that's a euphemism for quite stupid, I think.' (Martin O'Neill)

'Southampton here, down by the Solent, decidedly all at sea.' (Ian Browne, Radio 5 Live)

'Poborsky's had one or two moments. Two actually.' (Des Lynam)

Managers, however, cannot afford a string of poor performances. 'Everyone deserves five, six or seven chances but after 77 you blot your copy book,' remarked Martin O'Neill in explaining the omission of Frank Sinclair from the Leicester City Worthington Cup Final squad. Under threat, managers sometimes feel more secure in selecting reliable workhorses. They may avoid the players who light up the game. They don't play the skilful, creative talent for fear of their unpredictability. With a lack of creativity comes the measured game, the percentage pass, predictability and monotony: no inventiveness, but telegraphed passes. Not so much total football as bread-and-butter football. There's nothing hidden, no surprise. You just know what's coming.

The inventive footballer alarms and terrifies his manager, but such players strike the crowd with awe. Rob Steen said they 'scare managers with their quest for freedom – from fear, convention, boredom – and petrify them when they attain it'. The manager's fear of the creative, gifted, visionary player is a fear of unpredictability. Can they be relied upon? 'The maverick player might help you win, but he might also help you lose,' said Terry Venables, putting his finger on why so few creative players are picked for England. When they are, they are invariably converted into a less imaginative animal. Hence what happened to 'Butch' (Ray) Wilkins. Rob Steen commented that, 'He mellowed early and settled for the armchair... Joe Public came to scoff, to sneer at his peerless mastery of the square pass, of crab-ball. He seldom did anything wrong in an England shirt, but then rarely did he do much of a positive hue.'

This creates teams with no desire to entertain. Individual talent is obliterated. As George Graham said at Leeds United, 'We may lack creativity, but we make up for that in total commitment.' David Hopps noted that, under Walter Smith, Everton 'will forever imagine that they can coerce opponents into submission rather than outwit them'.

Chapter 4

Fitness

The modern footballer is lean, athletic, honed to muscular perfection and as fit as a robber's dog. They carry as much fat as a skeleton. Ron Atkinson said of Gordon Strachan as he came to the end of his playing career: 'There's nobody fitter at his age – except maybe Raquel Welch.' Maintaining a level of fitness in the modern game is crucial. The seemingly endless devotion to runs, shuttles and sprints that occupy so many training sessions epitomises this thinking. Fitness is the foundation for everything else. Ivan Golac suggested that 'A professional shouldn't be anything else but fit, so there's no hard work in just being able to run. The hard work comes when you have to play with imagination.'

But there are exceptions: lardies who wallow languidly in midfield or the paunchy rotunds labouring on the far reaches of the wing. Thomas Brolin briefly decorated the Leeds midfield with his portly presence. Jan Molby, as Brian Glanville suggested, 'looked corpulent enough to be playing darts for Denmark'. Goalkeepers who can fill the goal have perhaps more of an excuse. However, even Alex Ferguson was taken aback by the size of his goalie when he took charge of East Stirling. He said, 'Three weeks before kick-off I had eight players and a 15-stone goalkeeper who insisted he had done pre-season training.'

Paul Gascoigne struck fear into his new manager at Lazio, Dino Zoff, when a topless picture of the rogue at a night-club was shown to him. Zoff said, 'I only hope it's someone else's body with his face painted on.' He was to be proved sadly wrong. Linford Christie thought, 'Our shot-putters are in better condition than Gazza', yet Paul himself has a provocative explanation for his demeanour, suggesting, 'I've been told that I retain a lot of moisture when I eat.' Brian Clough defended his portly winger, John Robertson, by claiming, 'He was fatter than I was, but he

used to treat a football better than most people treat a woman.'
That's OK then. Wigan Athletic's Graeme Jones has a less
convincing spin. He explained, 'I wouldn't say I'm overweight but
I would say I'm too heavy.' Now that's one we can buy into.

Built on to the foundation of fitness, a player's physical attributes may be colloquially considered in terms of the 'S' factors:
suppleness, speed, strength, steel and stamina.

Suppleness

Outfield players require flexibility; goalkeepers need agility. Barry
Davies, in suggesting that 'Asprilla seems to have more joints than
other players', is probably endeavouring to make a point about
the Colombian's loose limbs. John Motson, in observing 'Seaman,
just like a falling oak, manages to change direction', applies a
perhaps less appropriate metaphor.

Suppleness tends to desert players as they age, as Glenn Hoddle
helpfully intimated in suggesting that 'When a player gets to 30, so
does his body.' Some players, however, stiff, awkward and inflex-
ible, seem never to have demonstrated pliancy in their limbs, as
Nigel Spink indicated in his description of his Aston Villa
goalkeeping colleague, Les Sealey: 'The last thing you could say
about Les is that he is a natural athlete.'

Speed

Pace, as we often hear, is frightening. It has become endemic in the
modern game. Everything is done at an accelerated pace. 'The way
everyone plays football now, the man will soon be moving faster
than the ball,' said coach Juan Lozano. Bobby Robson took it one
step further and suggested that the player will move, not only
quicker than the ball, but quicker than himself: 'He's ever so fast
and if he gets ahead of himself, nobody will catch him.'

A player with the ball at his feet flying past a stranded defender
lights up the stadium. 'Cyrille Regis was built like a cruiser-weight
and had the pace, near enough anyway, of an Olympic sprinter,'
said Ron Atkinson. 'Johan Cruyff's so fast over ten and twelve
yards that if he gets the ball first and you're more than six yards

from him, he'll leave you for dead,' observed Derek Johnstone.

Metaphors, some a tad obtuse, abound in depicting the speed of the quickest:

'Ian Rush is as quick as a needle.' (Ron Jones)

'Kanchelskis is getting quicker and fitter with every game.
He's up to about warp factor four at the moment.'
(Joe Royle)

'Stanley Matthews was like greased lightning.'
(Jack Charlton)

'Jurgen Klinsmann's like greased lightning in front of goal.'
(David Platt, rolling out a familiar metaphor)

'Julian Joachim: the diminutive striker with the cheetah's pace.' (Louise Taylor)

'Peter Osgood: built like a young poplar and blessed with an ease of movement that suggested castors had been glued to his feet at birth.' (Rob Steen)

'Les Ferdinand: blessed with supersonic acceleration, he can cover the first ten yards quicker than most defenders can blink.' (*Four Four Two*)

'Laurie Cunningham: an unquestioned master of running at pace with the ball and beating opponents as if they were merely a mirage.' (Ron Atkinson)

'They called Steve Kindon "the Horse" because of his speed. It was also because he had the brain of a clothes horse and the control of a rocking horse.' (Paul Fletcher)

A change of pace can be equally stunning. Ian St John described the Arsenal winger as 'Overmars in overdrive'. *Four Four Two* magazine suggest that Stoichkov's change of pace is all the more devastating 'because of the stupor in which he seems to spend so much of the game'.

In contrast to the man with pace is the lumbering plod of meat who is burnt off by the merest hint of a run from the opposing forward. Ron Atkinson refers to such players as 'lightning slow'. Pace, like other physical attributes, fades with advancing years. Glenn Hoddle noted that 'Stoichkov's legs have started to go a bit because he always had that explosive pace.' Steve Bruce made a dodgy denial of the relationship between age and lack of pace: 'Everyone said that I was picking up so many bookings last season because I was getting slower. That wasn't true. If I'd got any slower I'd have come to a standstill.' Yet Teddy Sheringham put a positive spin on his slothfulness by suggesting that, 'If I'd been two yards quicker, but not in my head, I might have been finished by now.'

Metaphors of the slow-footed include:

'Vinnie Jones is as ponderous as a carthorse.' (Jeff Powell)
'John Robertson: a heavily sedated three-toed sloth could have sprinted down the touchline with more gusto.' (Paul Simpson and Ray Spiller)
'Andy Neil was as slow as a funeral.' (Herbert Chapman, the great Arsenal manager)

Strength

Those strong in body and mind inherit the football pitch. The weak-bodied, skinny-legged version is unlikely to last very long in the top divisions. Dave Hill said, 'Pelé had a body of steel and a mind like a steel door.' Players who remain at the top for any length of time are durable, powerful and robust. They out-muscle the opposition, resist being pushed around and assert their presence on the field. This is reflected in the way Sir Matt Busby described the free-scoring Evertonian Dixie Dean: 'He had immense strength; adept on the ground but with extraordinary skill in the air. He was resilient in the face of the big, tough centre-halves of his day.' Of a centre-forward with a perhaps less free-scoring disposition, West Ham manager Harry Redknapp remarked: 'When Hartson goes for a cross, everything ends up in the back of the net – the ball, the centre-half and the goalkeeper.' Micky Adams, manager of Fulham, noted the need for an extra dimension in the nether regions of the league: 'You need a special type of footballer in the lower divisions – big and strong and nasty.'

'If that's Junior Baiano, I wouldn't like to meet Senior Baiano,' said Ron Atkinson on the Brazilian man mountain. However, with a few notable exceptions – Emile Heskey and Sol Campbell being two – not many players exhibit the physique of a Mike Tyson or Lennox Lewis. They display their strength more subtly. 'Kenny Dalglish wasn't that big but he had a huge arse. It came down below his knees and that's where he got his strength from,' noted Brian Clough.

Even the small and seemingly slight of build can be deceptively powerful. 'Zola is remarkably strong. You can close mark him, as several teams have elected to do, but you will never bully him out of the game,' said team-mate Craig Burley. 'Alan Hudson was a lot stronger than he looked – it was like hitting a barn door,' said Terry Venables after a challenge for the ball

Strength metaphors characteristically relate to the power and toughness of animals, old oak trees, fighting machines and brick walls:

'Colin Hendry can play football without legs. He's built like a young bull.' (Bill Fox)

'Stan Cullis was as strong as an ox. He would hurt you in the tackle.' (Stanley Matthews)

'Jaap Stam is like Steve Bould on roller skates ... he's as strong as a tree trunk, but more mobile.' (David Pleat)

'Pat Jennings has the strength of an SAS squaddie.' (Eamonn Dunphy)

'Daniel Amokachi's built like an ebony outhouse.' (Patrick Barclay)

Steel

'Soccer is a man's game, not an outing for namby-pambies,' said Jack Charlton. Dave 'Harry' Bassett made a similar point in stating, 'I don't want my players behaving like poofters. I want them to be men.' Hard men take the knocks. They ruggedly compete for the ball, bite in the tackle, and stand up to the most desperate and lunging neck-high tackles without a flinch. 'John McGrath would even play in short sleeves in the frost,' said an almost admiring Stan Bowles.

Hard men differ from the dirty player through having the ball, not the man, in mind, a point made by Tommy Smith, the notorious hard man in the centre of the Liverpool defence: 'I think the difference between being hard and dirty is that you go out to actually assault people. Being just hard you go out to play the game.' Survival, as Mark Hughes announced, depends on developing a tough character: 'I had to find the cut-throat meanness to survive in soccer.'

'I don't know how you define the word "hard man" … It's the media that gives you the label. My definition of myself would be a tough all-rounder,' said Vinnie Jones. George Best provides a different slant on hardness, but equally revealing, when describing his ball-winning midfielder: 'Nobby Stiles had a reputation for being hard but it was the way he played that made him hard to get the better of.' A further insight, provided by Gary Speed after a barracking by Leeds fans, suggests it is linked to physical appearance: 'If I was a skinhead Yorkshire-man and had tattoos and went around kicking people I'd be all right.'

Tommy Smith made a stab at a definition, saying, 'You look after yourself in football.' This comes independent of size. The unwary can be deceived. 'When you come up against a big fellow, and he doesn't realise you've got this streak of steel inside you, he's apt to think you're a pushover. Until the first real tackle – then, he suddenly realises that you may not have brawn, but you do possess bite,' observed Billy Bremner, the tiger in Leeds United's midfield.

And hard men are not afraid to display this side of their character to other hard men. 'I played the game hard. I gave some clumps and took my lumps,' said Jimmy Guthrie. This is reiterated by Graeme Souness's thoughts on Johnny Giles: 'If there was the slightest chance of Giles being hurt you would suddenly be confronted by a full set of studs.'

Hard men play a role. They perceive themselves, and are perceived by others, as hard and will defend that 'honour' unremittingly. 'Colin Hendry is one of those guys who isn't happy unless he's been kicked three times in the bollocks in training,' said Graeme Le Saux. Ron 'Chopper' Harris, the renowned Chelsea hard case, pertinently reflected: 'I don't really mind that I'm only remembered as a bloke who went in hard. It's better than not being remembered at all. 'Tommy Smith made a similar point: 'I spent 12 months building myself a reputation for hardness, and the next 12 years trying to get rid of it.'

Again the metaphors:

'Roy Keane's as hard as nails and doesn't give you a moment of peace.' (Gary Speed)

'Davie Sinclair is so hard he's got tattoos on his teeth.' (Jimmy Nicholl)

'Ceri Hughes's got the bite of a Mike Tyson. He'll eat the opposition, but there won't be anything left to spit out.' (Sam Hammam)

Stamina

Often referred to as having the legs to run all day, the lungs to work your butt off or excessive outpourings of perspiration, stamina or work rate is an attribute much prized by managers. Ron Atkinson noted that Laurie Cunningham, his prodigy at West Bromwich Albion, 'had phenomenal skill and yet, for such a creative player, he didn't leave you short on the sweat quotient either'. Some players will amaze even the most demanding of managers. Mick Jones, manager at Plymouth Argyle, paid Carlo Corazzin the following compliment: 'the work rate Carlo puts in defies science'. Others, less familiar with Einstein's theories of energy, resort to metaphor, as evidenced by Jim Baxter's comment on the contribution of Alan Ball, who 'was running about, demented, like a fart in a bottle'.

Stamina is a prerequisite of greatness. 'One thing all great players have in common is that they are prepared to work hard for the team,' noted Terry Venables. In Britain work rate is valued highly, a lesson that players from abroad readily discover and to which they have to adapt quickly if they are to become successful. 'I've learned things from being in England. I've discovered how to give more than 100%,' said Emmanuel Petit, perhaps a little tongue in cheek.

Players with stamina roll up their sleeves, run all day and graft. They contribute to the team: 'Colin Bell did the work of two men, as if he had an extra lung,' said Jimmy Greaves. They are valued by team members and the manager alike. 'Steve Watson's a real grafter. The only thing he ever suffers from is sweat rash,' claimed John Gregory, his manager at Aston Villa. Players who run non-stop create opportunities for others. They also put themselves in good positions: 'Technically Klinsmann is not a brilliant player, but he will always score because of his industry and persistence,' said Gunther Netzer.

Players lacking work rate are often perceived as flawed. Andy Gray, now a TV pundit, sought to draw awareness to David Ginola's contribution by suggesting, 'It's not what Ginola does when he's got the ball, it's what he doesn't do when he hasn't got it.' Work rate is independent of ball possession. Sometimes players attribute a lack of stamina to causes beyond their control. Stan Collymore, in saying 'I'm giving it my best shot, although there are times I wish I was born with more stamina', is proposing a genetic explanation. Whether many others endorse this view is, however, debatable. Perhaps not the coaches and physical trainers who schedule phases of running into the training programme to build up stamina. Most managers treat a lack of effort disdainfully, as when Ron Atkinson described Dalien Atkinson, his striker at Aston Villa, as 'An immensely talented footballer but somebody for whom the words "work" and "rate" didn't link.'

However, many players overcome a lack of stamina or work rate through their contributions to the team in other ways. Firstly, by their presence: 'Peter Reid can't run, can barely breathe, his legs have gone all soft and he can't kick a ball more than 10 yards. Yet look what he does. He calms everyone down. It's just what we needed,' said Mick Walker on signing him for Notts County. Secondly by their ability: 'Hagi's a lazy sod, but he can't half play,' said Terry Yorath. 'It's fair to say I was never a big believer in unnecessary exertion,' admitted Alan Hansen, who could defend by his masterly anticipation and reading of the game. Or finally, by their eye for a goal, as Jimmy Greaves, great goal-poacher, testifies: 'Work rate hardly existed in my vocabulary.' Reporter Ian Wooldridge elucidated: 'Jimmy Greaves used to hang around like a substitute best man at a wedding for 85 minutes and still win more matches than any other player.'

And as with all physical attributes, stamina fades with the advancing years. 'It's a terrible feeling when you've once been paid to keep fit and then you lose it. It's a sobering thought when you climb the stairs and you're out of breath,' aptly noted Martin Buchan, formerly of Manchester United.

Chapter 5

Talent

There is a pervasive perception that British footballers lack the technical quality of players from Europe and South America. As Florian Albert unhesitatingly remarked: 'In Hungary we make love to the ball and we sleep with it. The English eat it.' Players with superb technical ability do appear to cherish possession, caress the ball in their control and stroke rather than pass the ball. As the Scottish Don Juan and forward Jim Baxter advised, 'Treat the ball like a woman. Give it a cuddle, caress it a wee bit, take your time, and you'll get the right response.' Whether the phenomenon is continental or driven from the British game is open to debate. That fewer technically skilled players survive in the British game is perhaps due to a number of factors:

- The coaching of young players with an emphasis on competing and winning rather than playing for enjoyment.
- The inclement weather which encourages effort, graft and stamina in order to endure boggy and muddy pitches.
- Coaching that fosters work rate and running rather than technical and ball skills. Rangers boss Walter Smith made exactly this point in suggesting that 'kids learn to play the game of football rather than learn to play football ... Even at under-10 level they learn to play the offside trap and nonsense like that.'
- The demands of the British game which is fast, passionate and full of challenges and does not allow players to have time on the ball.
- The attitude of some British managers that ball players are a luxury, not team players, and likely to let the side down.

There are pockets within the British game that encourage the pursuit of technique. Traditionally West Ham have fostered cultured play, Nottingham Forest and Aston Villa relied on skilful attack and Liverpool emphasise a passing game. Crewe Alexandra, under Dario Gradi, play a refined style of football because in that way they believe they can win. 'Football is a game of skill, not combat,' claims Gradi.

Remarkably some skilful players survive and flourish in spite of the anti-skill culture. As Steve Claridge so eloquently remarked, 'Defenders are like tradesmen, strikers are the craftsmen. People don't pay money to watch centre-half cloggers kicking shit out of the centre-forward, do they?'

This chapter explores the aspects of technique that define the complete footballer:

Ball control

Nwankwo Kanu, the Arsenal forward, was described by Simon Turnbull as having 'a gazelle-like stealth and a sublime touch'. A great touch creates time and space. Graham Taylor made the point that 'time and space are the same thing', which might unnerve the astrophysicists caught up in the fourth dimension, but the link is undoubtedly true on the football pitch.

Players who have been applauded for their touch, control and feel for the ball include:

'The only four letter word to do with Bobby Moore was *time*; he just had all the time in the world.' (Bobby Gould)

'John Barnes has the ability, almost inexplicable, to contrive a fragment of space when hemmed in on the by-line.' (Dave Hill)

'Franco Baresi's on first name terms with the ball.' (Azeglio Vicini, Italy manager)

'George Weah has a delicate touch that belies his awesome physique.' (*Four Four Two*)

Paul Gascoigne: 'The velcro-like control is still there, but even a sublime first touch cannot disguise his inability to surge past markers in the manner of old.' (Louise Taylor)

Raich Carter: 'I never saw Raich under pressure. He carried space around him like an umbrella.' (Willie Watson)

Players with great control master the conditions. 'There was no such thing as a bumpy pitch as far as Stan Bowles was concerned. He always killed the ball stone dead,' said Frank McLintock.

Those bereft of touch and control treat the ball as a leper. They let the ball make a fool of them. They let it bounce, squirm under their foot, or control it with a shin or knee; they seem utterly perplexed by its spin and pace, and they get rid of it as soon as possible. They are forever in a rush and under pressure. Such players have to compensate in other ways for their fear of the ball:

Steve Bull: 'People say his first touch isn't good, but he usually scores with his second.' (Graham Turner, his manager at Wolves)

'Carlton Palmer covers every blade of grass on the pitch – mainly because his first touch is crap.' (Dave Jones, his manager at Southampton)

'Mark Hateley couldn't trap a dead rat.' (Stan Bowles)

'Gary Megson couldn't trap a land mine.' (Brian Clough)

'When Geoff Thomas traps the ball it goes as far as I used to be able to kick it.' (George Best)

Vinnie Jones: 'If I were to test him on things like controlling the ball, passing, moving after passing, I would have to fail him and send him back to the building site.' (Alan Hudson)

Two-footed

'Being naturally right footed, he doesn't often chance his arm with the left foot,' observed Trevor Brooking, mixing a collection of appendages. Having two good feet may seem essential, yet some very good players rely on only one, using their 'spare leg' for standing on. Jimmy Hill made this point in a less than clear summary of David Beckham: 'He has two feet, which a lot of people say players don't have these days.'

'My left foot is not one of my best,' mused Sammy McIlroy. The question is, did he do anything to improve it? George Best hints at what made him a wizard with both feet: 'I kept working on my left foot until it actually became stronger than my right one.' This is perhaps a simple formula for overcoming weaknesses, but in practice it is rarely pursued for long. But here is a puzzle – a player who is unaware of his main attribute. 'I've always been comfortable at left back. The left foot has helped – it's always been there, but I haven't always had the chance to use it,' said Stig Inge Bjornebye, Liverpool's Norwegian wing-back.

The left peg invariably seems to be aesthetically more pleasing. When speaking about Jason Wilcox, Mark Lawrenson's inadvertent comment was: 'Most players would give their right arm for his left foot.' John Gregory enthused over his new midfield acquisition, Alan Thompson: 'I've always loved left-footed players. There's something about them that's very sexy.' Mick Mills of Ipswich Town, similarly in awe of the leftie, said of Frank Worthington, 'He had tremendous touch, a lovely left foot. Like left-handed tennis players, left-footed footballers seem better to look at. Frank not only was good, he looked good.'

The left foot evokes some intriguing descriptions:

'That Gheorghe Hagi has got a left foot like Brian Lara's bat.'
(Don Howe)
'Gheorghe Hagi: he's got a great left foot. He could open a can of beans with that foot.' (Ray Clemence)
'Ferenc Puskas's left foot was like a hand – he could do anything with it. In the showers he would even juggle with the soap.' (Francisco Gento)
'Steve Staunton's left foot is so good he could open a jar of pickles with it.' (John Gregory, Aston Villa)
'Julian Dicks has a great left foot – it's like a cannon.'
(Billy Bonds)
'I've always said to Paul [Furlong]: thank God you haven't got a right foot as well, because then you would've cost me £4.6 million.' (Matthew Harding)

Even right-footed players are astonished when something left-sided comes off. 'I've been playing 15 years and it's only today I realised that I'm left footed,' marvelled Dave Watson, of Everton, after a 25-yard left-foot screamer hit the onion bag and saved a point at Arsenal.

Keeping possession

'There are only two basic situations in football. Either you have the ball or you don't,' stated Ron Greenwood emphatically. When you have the ball, keeping it should be a prime motive. The aim should be to restrict the opposition's possession to picking it out of the net. 'For me the ball is a diamond. If you have a diamond you don't get rid of it, you offer it,' commented Glenn Hoddle.

Possession is maintained by shielding the ball, holding off challenges, laying it off, and passing to team-mates. Those able to demonstrate this include:

'Tom Finney told me that if I got tired I should play the ball
  out to him on the wing and he would keep hold of it until I
  got my breath back. He did it too.' (Bobby Robson)
Carlos Valderama: 'I thought he was a bit lazy, a luxury
  player, but getting the ball off him … it took three of us
  at one point.' (Graeme Le Saux)

Passing

'Stephen McPhail's got a terrible habit of passing to his team-mates,' bemoaned David O'Leary of Leeds United. Simple accurate passing maintains possession. An advanced diploma in geometry sometimes helps with measured passes to feet, a one–two interplay, playing in triangles to create space, or the bread-and-butter percentage ball. Some players, such as Michael Duberry of Chelsea, make this their goal. Duberry said, 'I've got to play to my strengths. If I can give a simple five-yard pass to a blue shirt, then that's my job done.'

Passes create chances: incisive, rapier-like balls that cut through the defence; balls threaded through on an angle; through balls arrowed into the path of an on-running forward; chipped passes played into space behind the defence. The intelligent ball is the one that does the damage. Players distinguished by their devastating passing include:

Ruud Gullit: 'He can destroy you with one pass.' (Joe Jordan)

Ruud Gullit: 'He plays the short passes with carefree simplicity and the long range missiles with uncanny accuracy.' (Harry Harris)

Nigel Clough: 'He can unlock a defence with a cunning pass, an intelligently weighted short pass.' (Dave Sexton)

Johnny Giles: 'He was the finest passer of a ball I have ever come across. I used to marvel at him. He enthralled me. He was so accurate that it was like using a billiard cue. He made passing a simple exercise.' (Pat Partridge, referee)

Paul McGrath: 'He distributes the ball like a gifted midfielder.' (Terry Venables)

Gunther Netzer: 'There was a magnetic precision about his passing, from 40 yards or four – weight, timing, angles – the lot.' (Rob Steen)

Gunther Netzer: 'He was a bit more direct in that he would play it and go, whereas I tended to spray my passes.' (Tony Currie)

Tony Currie: 'Sometimes his passes were fantastic, but by the time they got there they weren't always as dangerous as the little ones.' (Alan Hudson)

John Barnes: 'With his left foot Barnes can deliver the ball with startling accuracy, swirling it towards onrushing colleagues in great, looping parabolas.' (Dave Hill)

Ray Wilkins: 'And Wilkins sends an inch-perfect pass … to no one in particular.' (Bryon Butler)

Crossing is a particular skill, rarely completed accurately and consistently by any player. More usually, they are skewed into the stand or resemble Kate Moss, as Mark Lawrenson put it, in being a little behind the forward run. Quality crosses arrive short at the near post or deep on to the far peg. They are floated, driven or whipped in to create mayhem amongst defenders. That few players acquire the skill is borne out by the following thoughts:

'You can only wonder at some of the things Di Canio does.
  Now, can he do the simple things like cross the ball …?'
  (Jon Champion)
José Dominguez: 'I love him, everybody loves him. But when
  you analyse what he does, his final ball is crap. Full stop'.
  (Barry Fry)

Dribbling

A lost art. The man who skips past a rooted defender, ghosts past
a challenge, runs at a startled clogger, sucks a defender in and
then drags the ball away, skins the marker on the outside or
nutmegs a bewildered full back is immediately a hero. 'Good
players know when to make a move and how to beat an
opponent,' said Wilf Mannion. David Ginola said, 'I love to run
with the ball. One day I won't be running any longer. But I will
run fast while I can.'

Rodney Marsh flags up a benefit of taking defenders on – the
possibility of a free kick when the tackle is mistimed: 'I always
keep the ball close when I'm dribbling – never more than a foot
away. So if the fellow doesn't get the ball, he gets me.'

Some of the top players with the ball at their feet:

Romario: 'The only player I know who can dribble within a
  square metre.' (Johan Cruyff)
Stanley Matthews: 'Playing Stan is like playing a ghost.'
  (Johnny Carey)
Stanley Matthews: 'He was as tricky as a wagon load of
  monkeys, and you never got a clue which way he was
  going.' (Norman Greehalgh, Everton)
Rodney Marsh: 'He would run at fellas, looking at them and
  chatting to them while dribbling the ball between his heels.'
  (Alec Stock, QPR)
Ossie Ardiles: 'He was the difference – it was like trying to
  tackle dust.' (Joe Royle)
John Barnes: 'He runs with the ball and commits opponents,
  expects to win some and lose some, to trade errors for the
  confusion he prompts.' (Dave Hill)

Bebeto: 'He was going at 100 mph. These guys are dribbling maniacs.' (Alexi Lalas)

Chris Waddle: 'For a defender, Chris running at you is the worst sight in football.' (Mark Lawrenson)

Ruel Fox: 'He's like a bar of soap. When he's on song, it's difficult to nail him down.' (Dave Stringer, Norwich City)

John Barnes: 'He likes to give his ass a shake and swerve his way past three men and still have the ball.' (Dave Hill)

Wilf Mannion: 'Nobody ever got near him to kick him. He didn't have to be tough. When people tackled him he seemed to ride everything. He just floated over the turf.' (Alan Peacock)

Peter Osgood: 'With a casually deceptive amble ... that sinuous shift which took him past an opponent who, left with a baffled look on his face, turned to gaze almost in awe.' (Tommy Docherty)

And a contrast:

'Milosevic spat at the fans. Collymore can't even dribble.' (Richard Littlejohn)

Feints

To drop a shoulder at pace and see a defender completely sold by the dummy so that he lunges into fresh air is a satisfying experience. 'Don't ask me to describe it [the body swerve]. It just comes out of me under pressure,' said the maestro, Stanley Matthews. Frank McAvennie, in describing Kenny Dalglish, alludes to a potential benefit: 'Kenny was one of the dirtiest players I've ever seen. Not in a bad sense. But he had this way of shimmying and drawing players into fouls. It was usually deliberate and amazing to watch.' Other masters of selling dummies include:

Liam Brady: 'His trademark dropping of the left shoulder always deceived.' (*Four Four Two*)

Eddie Colman: 'When he waggled his hips he made the stanchions in the grandstand sway.' (Harry Gregg)

Charlie Cooke: 'When he sold you a dummy, you had to pay to get back into the ground.' (Jim Baxter)

Romario: 'On the edge of the box he comes alive: feinting, shimmying, twisting, turning ... he has a repertoire of tricks that would be the envy of David Copperfield.'
(*Four Four Two*)

Gianfranco Zola: 'He had space and time ... shimmying about as if he had no bones.' (Rick Gekoski)

Balance

Balance gives players the rhythm, grace and fluency to ride tackles. George Best, himself so wonderfully composed and balanced, remarked on the attribute: 'Gullit, Maradona, Pelé, Beckenbauer, Cruyff: they all had excellent balance and if you are going in for a tackle or challenging for a 50/50 ball, the player with the better balance stands a better chance. He's going to be on his feet, not off them.'

Those with balance include:

Pat Jennings: 'He has the grace of a ballet dancer.' (Eamonn Dunphy)

Denis Law: 'He could dance on egg shells.' (Bill Shankly)

Eddie Gray: 'When he plays on snow, he doesn't leave any footprints.' (Don Revie)

Juninho: 'He moves like a gazelle. He will sense the rhinos are coming.' (Wilf Mannion)

Peter Osgood: 'Gliding across the muddy morass at Turf Moor, a gazelle on skis, Peter evaded four challenges before rounding off a solo sally of such outrageous panache that even the Burnley keeper, Adam Blacklaw applauded him back to the centre circle.' (Rob Steen)

George Best: 'He survives only because his incredible balance allows him to ride with the impact of some of the tackles he has to take.' (Sir Matt Busby)

George Best: 'No one I ever played with or saw, could ride a tackle better than George Best. He was simply the greatest player of my time.' (Terry Neill)

George Best: 'He had a devastating change of pace, a change of direction perhaps better than anyone, balance so marvellous that he could be almost falling to the ground before coming back up again.' (Terry Venables)

Movement

Often unnoticed and sometimes referred to as unselfish, movement off the ball opens up attacking possibilities. Runs create space for others. Good players peel away from their markers, overlap down the wing, run along the line, pull a defender out of position for others to exploit the space:

Alan Shearer: 'He shakes off central defenders like ill fitting jackets.' (Guy Hodgson)

John Charles: 'He can shake off opponents as a dog shakes water off its back.' (H.D. 'Donny' Davies)

Ian Wright: 'He was at his most slippery, luring defenders to come close into his back, then peeling away.' (Kevin McCarra)

Gianluca Vialli: 'He's the best in the country at running off the ball.' (Harry Redknapp)

Effective, goal-creating runs often start deep, with players stealing into the penalty box from midfield, or arriving late and unnoticed for a free header:

John Charles: 'Everything John does is automatic. When he moves into a position for a goal chance it is instinctive. I do not posses his intuitiveness. His feet do his thinking.' (Danny Blanchflower)

Gustavo Poyet: 'He's a big strong player and when he arrives in the box on those late runs he's very dangerous, especially in the air.' (Jamie Redknapp)

Jurgen Klinsmann: 'He's very elusive, a real thinking man's footballer.' (Kit Symons)

Heading

Headers can be cushioned, directed or powerful. They can be
flicked on from the near post or headed back across goal. Great
headers of the ball time their jump and appear to hang in the air.
They relish an aerial challenge, or put their noddle in with flying
boots and studs, stretching for a glorious diving header.

> Liam Daish: 'He would jump up and head a jumbo jet away if
> it was threatening our goal.' (Barry Fry, Birmingham City)
> Paul McGrath: 'He seems to have a magnetic head – every-
> thing comes to him.' (Andy Townsend, Aston Villa)
> Lee Mills: 'He's the best attacker of the ball in the air in the
> division. But that is probably down to his lack of brains.'
> (Stuart Talbot, Port Vale)

Others seem a tad more hesitant in sticking their heads in:

> Darren Huckerby: 'I told him we had some shampoo in the
> dressing room if he wanted to get his head dirty.' (Gordon
> Strachan, Coventry City)
> 'The problem with Jason Lee having that lump on top of his
> head [the infamous "pineapple" hairstyle] is that I'm not
> sure he knows which angle the ball will come off.' (Frank
> Clark, Nottingham Forest)

Goal sense

Those who can finish are lethal. They are assassins of the box.
They remain composed, stealthily anticipate where the ball will be
and, with the whites of the goal in sight, strike with deadly
accuracy. Juninho descriptively makes the point, saying, 'Some
people become blind when they get close to the goal. Gascoigne
doesn't. See the goal he scored against Scotland in Euro '96. If you
were watching the match from the outside that seemed the
obvious, the only thing to do. Things are different when you're in
there.' And that's where you see the outstanding player – calm and
cold-blooded at decisive moments.

The feeling of scoring is frequently and aptly describes as orgasmic. 'Scoring is my life,' said Gabriel Batistuta. 'A nice dribble or a back heel means nothing to me. All that counts is sticking the ball in the back of the net.' And it does not appear to matter quite how a goal is scored. 'They don't bother to describe them in the record books. They just count them,' commented Jimmy Greaves, renowned for being in the right place at the right time in the 18-yard box, playing down merits of the 25-yard screamer that ricochets off the bar into the net. The fan, however, begs for a goal but cherishes a blinder.

Strikers have variously been assessed in terms of:

- the number of touches they need: 'Tony Yeboah: it's not his goals to games ratio, it's his goals to touches that impresses me' (Joe Royle);
- goals per chance ratio: 'Andy Cole's problem is that he still needs three or four opportunities in front of goal before he takes one' (Glenn Hoddle); or
- goals per game ratio: at international level Gerd Muller's 68 goals in 62 games is a tremendous ratio; Ferenc Puskas netted 83 goals in 84 games for Hungary; Pelé found the onion bag 79 times in 92 appearances.

Top strikers ping the ball, they shoot with venom, and dip or slot the ball accurately inside the post:

Alan Shearer: 'He was the best striker I've ever faced, without question – and that was only in training.' (David May at Blackburn Rovers)

John Aldridge: 'He knew the angles and anxieties of the penalty area intimately.' (Dave Hill)

Tony Yeboah: 'He knows where that 192 square feet of net is, and normally he hits it.' (Howard Wilkinson)

Ronaldo: 'He's unstoppable in the box. It doesn't matter how tightly defenders mark him, he'll find a way past and his finishing is lethal.' (Bobby Robson)

Ally McCoist: 'You're like dogshit in the penalty box. We don't know you're there until the damage is done.' (John Hughes)

Tony Yeboah: 'His touch was immaculate – it was in the net
    in the time it takes a snowflake to melt on a hot stove.'
    (Howard Wilkinson)
John Barnes: 'He can bend a free kick around the most solid
    defensive walls and ping the ball into the roof of the net.'
    (Dave Hill)
Robbie Fowler: 'He was like a fox in that area, the way he
    hunted for his goals.' (Gerard Houllier, Liverpool)
Geoff Hurst: 'He had a hammer in his left boot.' (Jimmy
    Greaves)
Bobby Charlton: 'He releases rockets from the edge of the
    area that go home like a clap of thunder and lift the
    opposing net as if a gale had struck it.' (Geoffrey Green)
John Aldridge: 'The boy is a mean machine: a real gunfighter.
    It doesn't matter who you are he'll shoot you down when
    he's in the box.' (John King, Tranmere Rovers)
Ronald Koeman: 'Facing a Koeman free kick is like facing
    a serial killer.' (Archie McPherson)

And perhaps the not-so-competent snatch at shots, scuff the
turf, drag a sitter wide or balloon one over the bar from point-
blank range. Tommy Docherty once remarked that his strikers
couldn't score in a brothel:

Asa Harford: 'One of Asa's great qualities is not scoring
    goals.' (Roy Small)
Les Ferdinand: 'His only fault is his finishing.' (Trevor
    Brooking)
Carlton Palmer: 'He is the worst finisher since Devon Loch.'
    (Ron Atkinson)
Andy Cole: 'He's known as "jigsaw" because he goes to
    pieces in the box.' (Wimbledon match programme)
John Hartson: 'The striker struck like a toothless cobra.'
    (Martin Samuel)
'The shot from Laws was precise but wide.' (Alan Parry)

Marking

'They were marked by leeches of blue and white stripes,' noted David Pleat in applauding the Argentine defence during World Cup '98. Defenders set about shackling forwards, sticking to them like glue, keeping tight on wingers or man-marking the creative influence on the opposing side. Midfielders close men down, cover and press the opposition. Marking is one of the least glamorous activities demanded of players, but inevitably it is highlighted as a failure when a goal is conceded. Nowadays strikers are expected to mark a post or pick up a marauding centre-back in defending a corner. They are also expected to go with their man if he makes a run, but sometimes this occurs only with considerable reluctance and indifference. 'If you want someone to track back as well as do what I do, he would cost about £25 million,' reckoned Matt Le Tissier.

Ruud Gullit gave an insight into the experience of being in the defender's pocket when he said, 'In Italy I was man-marked all the time. I would go to the loo and they'd be waiting for me. I'd say while you're there, hold this will you.' From the defender's viewpoint, Vinnie Jones had a novel approach to marking Ruud Gullit: 'If all else fails, you could wait for the first corner and tie his dreadlocks to the goalpost.' John Carey provides a glimpse of the troublesome nature of marking a top-class striker: 'Playing against Stanley Matthews is like playing a ghost.'

Some of those who have mastered the art of marking include:

Martin Keown: 'He's up everybody's backside.' (Trevor Brooking)

Ron Harris: 'Imagine what he can do with his mind set – the ball could be there, two yards away, but all he wants to do is just stay here with me.' (Stan Bowles)

Lee Bowyer: 'He's closer to John Collins than John Collins's shirt.' (Stuart Hall)

Chris Perry: 'He's very mobile and a hard man to shake off.' (Martin Tyler)

Bobby Moore: 'He marked me on and off for fifteen years, and I couldn't even kick him once to unsettle his equilibrium or agitate him momentarily.' (Bobby Gould)

Nobby Stiles: 'He would be assigned on specific occasions to do a specific job and he did it better than anyone I have seen.' (George Best)

Defending

Huddersfield Town has the sorry distinction of being the only side ever to score six goals in a league match and still lose. In 1957 they were away at Charlton Athletic, leading 5–1 against ten men with 20 minutes left to play, and contrived to lose 7–6. 'Strikers win matches, but defenders win championships,' said John Gregory of Aston Villa, although divisions can be won on goals scored rather than least conceded: Arsenal came second in the race for the Premiership in 1999 despite conceding only 17 goals compared with Manchester United whose relatively leaky defence let in 37 goals. As Adrian Heath at Burnley suggested: 'We must tighten up at the back. I've told the lads we are not going to win many games 4–3.'

Class defenders have positional sense, anticipating where the ball will be played. They break up attacks by their interceptions. They block shots, cover, mop up, close players down and generally perceive problems before they arise. They often work in tandem with other defenders, pushing out together, holding the line and organising the play at free kicks. Bobby Moore, a master of defending, said, 'The art is to deny a forward space and force him to knock the ball away.'

Defending, some argue, is easier than being an attacker because normally the defender faces the ball. Intuitively defenders may feel less competent. They don't seek the glory and limelight that strikers might. 'I was never what you'd call a gifted player so I had to play to my strengths. And that involved stopping the other teams playing at all costs,' said Ron 'Chopper' Harris.

Yet top-class defending is of equal importance to a team's success. Holding a lead with ten minutes to go, or keeping a clean sheet away at Brentford, Norwich City or Leeds United is no mean feat.

The masters include:

Bobby Moore: 'To find a way past Bobby Moore was like searching for the exit from Hampton Court maze.' (David Miller)

Bobby Moore: 'Knowing that he lacked a sharp change of pace, he painstakingly programmed into his make up a positional sense which made it almost impossible for opponents to exploit that flaw.' (Jeff Powell)

Chris Perry: 'He's like a leech, so quick, and a brilliant defender.' (Alex Ferguson)

Rio Ferdinand: 'West Ham's defence works on the reverse sandwich principle. Ferdinand is the delicacy sandwiched between those two lumps of meat: Ruddock and Ian Pearce. They should call the back three here "Beauty and the Beasts".' (Paul Hayward)

Franco Baresi: 'I remember swopping jerseys with Franco Baresi. What was depressing was that he got a sweat-soaked Scotland number nine while the Italy number six I got in return was not only bone-dry but still smelling of his cologne.' (Ally McCoist)

And the less impressive defenders:

Rodney Marsh: 'He had a headache coming back over the halfway line.' (Dave Webb)

Paul Gascoigne: 'It is normal for Gazza that he is lacking in defensive phases.' (Zdenek Zeman, Lazio coach)

Tackling

'The art of tackling, as with many other things, is in the timing – the contact, winning the ball, upsetting the opposition, maybe even hurting them. You're in, you're out, you've won it and you've hurt him and left him lying there, but its not a foul,' summarised Bill Shankly.

Peter Storey of Arsenal eloquently defined the need for ball winners. He said, 'The sugar plum fairy could play centre-forward if it weren't for people like me.' Tackling involves tenacity, timing, a 'thou shalt not pass' attitude, keeping on your feet, snapping at the man with the ball, as in doing a 'doggie', and sliding in with precision. The ball should be won first and what subsequently happens to the man is irrelevant in terms of the laws of the game. Ron 'Chopper' Harris knew this well: 'I never saw myself as a dirty player. I'd always go for the ball. Quite often I'd take the man as well,' he said.

It demands technique and 'Nobody ever won a tackle with a smile on his face,' as Bruce Rioch noted. But a won tackle generates few better feelings, as Paul Ince revealed: 'I love tackling, love it. It's better than sex.'

Noted tacklers include:

Paul McGrath: 'He tackles like a tank trap.' (Terry Venables)

Norman Hunter: 'He doesn't tackle opponents so much as break them down for re-sale as scrap.' (Julie Welch)

Colin Hendry: 'He's great in the air, a superb tackler, and the best blocker I've ever seen.' (Alan Hansen)

Stan Bowles: 'He would get back and tackle and fight to the death.' (Dave Webb)

Steve McMahon: 'He was a bit of a rat in getting hold of the ball.' (Alan Hudson)

Jim Holton: 'A one-man grappling iron.' (David Meek)

Billy Bremner: 'Ten stone of barbed wire.' (*Sunday Times*)

Nobby Stiles: 'He was niggly, like a terrier, always at your heels. You couldn't knock him away.' (George Best)

Nobby Stiles: 'Every team needs a man with his capacity for work and the willingness to hustle and tackle in midfield.' (Francis Lee)

Bryan Robson: 'He has all the subtlety of a rhino, but see how he keeps winning the ball.' (Jim Baxter)

Anton Ondrus: 'He was a hard player … from the start his tackles and challenges in the air carried the force of a sledgehammer.' (Andy Gray)

Stuart McCall: 'He made it into the *Guinness Book of Records* for the world's longest slide tackle – he dispossessed a guy playing on another park.'

Some players, however, rely on others to win them the ball:

Bobby Charlton: 'He is not very good at winning the ball in midfield and has leaned heavily on Stiles in this respect. To put it another way, Stiles provides the bullets for Charlton to fire.' (Johnny Giles)

Glenn Hoddle: 'A cultured ball wizard who thought tackle was something you put in your fishing bag.' (Zit magazine)

Eric Cantona: 'He's not a tackler ... he doesn't know how to do it and usually ends up with a booking. Forwards aren't expected to tackle – they conserve themselves for scoring or creating.' (Alex Ferguson)

And some tackles are mistimed or non-existent:

'Good challenge by Wright, but an unfair one.' (Brian Moore)

'I couldn't tackle a fish supper. I think I only made one tackle in my life.' (Jim Baxter)

'We all genuinely go for the ball – it's just that sometimes we can miss it by quite a distance and unfortunately the tackle looks worse than it really was.' (Neil Ruddock)

Chapter 6

Presence

'It's psychological. When things are not right in
your head, they can't be right in your body.
Footballers are the same as everyone else.'
Emmanuel Petit

The Frenchman's quote reveals two important themes. The complete footballer dedicates himself to improving the psychological side of his game as much as the physical and technical sides. If any one of the triad is neglected, then the player's potential is reduced.

Petit's second point highlights the similarity of psychological functioning across each and every one of us, in terms of confidence, decision making, self-awareness, emotional control, concentration and so forth. These functions are important in enhancing our performance in everyday tasks. It would be difficult to rap dance without confidence, order fast food without making the odd decision, charm the sales assistant without a hint of self-awareness, give a lecture if you are a nervous wreck or follow a film if you have the attention of a deranged wasp.

The difference is that, to perform well, a footballer has to develop a heightened level of such functions. Many of the later chapters of this book specifically elaborate the central psychological functions, sometimes depicted as the 'Cs' – confidence, concentration and control – and this chapter develops a theme around presence, or the way in which a player can impose himself upon a game.

A player may possess a purely physical presence because of his size. 'Ron Yeats really frightened half the country out of playing by his sheer presence. A very, very good centre-half and certainly the hardest that I had to play against,' said Joe Royle. A similar point was alluded to in Paul Hall's description of the Portsmouth goalkeeper when he suggested that, 'Alan Knight is part of the furniture; like a grandad. He's a miserable old git, but he has such presence.' However, there are more psychological aspects to a player's influence on the game.

Intelligence

Few footballers would feel at ease in debating the merits of chaos theory or feel inclined to express a view on Wittgenstein's critique of his early works. 'I'm not the brainiest person. I ain't got no O-levels. Nothing. I didn't go back for my results. All I ever wanted to do was play football,' said Julian Dicks, without a shred of modesty. In a similar vein, Teddy Sheringham stated, not entirely convincingly, 'I don't know if I've got a footballing brain. I only got one O-level at school, but that was in PE Studies, so that helps I suppose.' There are of course exceptions. Andy Gray, TV analyst, was adamant in saying, 'Ruud Gullit knows far too much about football. We're not having him on again.'

Steve Ogrizovic, of Coventry City, insisted on a different perspective regarding intelligence, associating it with the quick-witted rather than the half-witted: 'If you're interested in intelligence, you'll find it in the piss-taking in the dressing room ... some of the guys are really quick and inventive.'

Intelligence, in the footballing vernacular, refers to a player's ability to read the game, spot the danger, have vision and aware-ness, see the pass and dictate the play through being at the hub of most good work. A snippet of advice from coach Malcolm Allison that Bobby Moore nurtured was to keep forever asking yourself: 'If I get the ball now, who will I give it to?' This one statement secured Moore the priceless gift of reading a game. 'I tried to read the game intelligently, holding back to mark space rather than a man, to win the ball by thinking first and moving first. My game was all about anticipation,' he remarked.

Those noted for their footballing brains include:

Michel Platini: 'Even his feet are intelligent.' (Michel Hidalgo, manager of France)

Juninho: 'He may be only 5'5" tall, but size does not count if you have a football brain.' (Wilf Mannion)

Johan Cruyff: 'He saw passes others couldn't see, picked up runs others wouldn't anticipate.' (*Four Four Two*)

Steve Nichol: 'He could sit in an arm chair and play, because he's got a brain.' (David Pleat)

Gianfranco Zola: 'His peripheral vision is so acute that he actually seems to respond to the runs of players arriving from behind him.' (Rick Gekoski)

Norman Whiteside: 'His game was all about intelligence, awareness and the perceptive pass. He could see the big picture. He knew exactly the position and availability of every player on the pitch at any given moment.' (Ron Atkinson)

Lother Matthäus: 'He conducts midfield like a latter day Sir Malcolm Sargent.' (Steve Curry)

Paul Merson: 'When he has the ball he can paint pictures.' (Bruce Rioch)

Jamie Redknapp: 'He is what I call a three-touch player and if he uses that you can't get near him because he sees the play early.' (Glenn Hoddle)

Alan Hudson: 'Where his brilliance lay was in recognising where the opposition's weaknesses were, getting the ball and servicing those who could best take advantage.' (Dave Webb)

Alan Hudson: 'He was always, always available. I've never known anyone to be more readily available.' (Dave Webb)

Alan Hudson: 'Prompting and probing with surgical exactitude, Alan mapped out moves three passes ahead.' (Rob Steen)

Bryan Robson: 'He seemed to anticipate where Terry Butcher's headers were going and get there first. He knew how and when to arrive in the right places at the right time.' (Tony Adams)

Paul McGrath: 'He reads the play like a clairvoyant.' (Terry Venables)

Didier Domi: 'He's a very good positional player ... if you're
  in the right position you don't need to tackle.' (Ruud Gullit)
Bobby Moore: 'The best reader of a football match in the
  world.' (Jeff Powell)
Kenny Dalglish: 'He had this rare quality of being able to
  know where the other players were without even looking
  and to find them with a perfect pass.' (Bob Paisley)
Jamie Redknapp: 'He ran the game like a ringmaster, passing
  the ball with geometric precision.' (Joe Lovejoy)
Phillipe Albert: 'He reads the game tremendously and then
  eats up the ground to get where he wants to be.' (Peter
  Beardsley)
Roger Byrne: 'He read the game brilliantly and took the
  whole field of play into perspective, always knowing where
  he should be.' (Sir Matt Busby)
David Platt: 'He is an extraordinarily intelligent player. Ten
  years ahead of his time.' (Gianluca Vialli, paraphrasing a
  well-worn English expression)

Then there are those who survive or, indeed, light up the game
without due attention to anticipation, peripheral vision or
thought, as Allan Clarke intimated in his comment, 'I don't think,
Brian. You don't think in this game.' It is, however, defenders who
periodically come into the spotlight for their lack of savvy, as
observed by Colin Hendry of Blackburn Rovers, who made the
less than complimentary remark that, 'People are going to think
that not only are centre-halves useless and ugly, but we're also
thick.' Some others who have been criticised in the grey matter
stakes include:

Paul Gascoigne: 'George Best without brains.' (Stan
  Seymour)
Paul Gascoigne: 'I once said Gazza's IQ was less than his
  shirt number and he asked me, "What's an IQ?"'
  (George Best)
Paul Gascoigne: 'I don't want to be rude about Gazza, but
  when God gave him this enormous footballing talent, he
  took his brains out at the same time.' (Tony Banks MP)

Paul Gascoigne: 'He's an intelligent boy who likes to let people think he's stupid.' (Ally McCoist)

Carlton Palmer: 'He never shuts up. Talks some rubbish but we throw that away and sometimes some intelligence comes out.' (Gordon Strachan)

Simon Tracey: 'He's got the brains of a rocking horse.' (Dave Bassett, Sheffield United)

Liverpool: 'My players had sawdust in their heads today.' (Bob Paisley, in the aftermath of a defeat by Chelsea)

Robert Prosinecki: 'He's been playing from memory … or maybe from amnesia.' (Ron Atkinson)

Cunning, intuition and speed of thought

Those who outwit the opposition through guile and sharp thinking are a rare breed. They include:

Johan Cruyff: 'He has amazing reflexes and likes to outfox his opposition mentally as well as physically. He'll lie doggo for a spell and you'll think he's not trying. Then suddenly he zooms in when you least expect it and he's scored.' (Derek Johnstone)

George Best: 'A son of instinct rather than logic.' (Geoffrey Green)

Jimmy Greaves: 'He could lose defenders by stealth and psychic game-reading.' (Sir Matt Busby)

Jimmy Greaves: 'He was the arch-pickpocket of goals.' (Geoffrey Green)

Jimmy Greaves: 'He will shoot about two seconds before I've even thought about it.' (Johnny Haynes)

Denis Law: 'He beat people by his speed of thought.' (Harry Gregg)

Juninho: 'He can control and pass, he's got a quick mind, he's small, he's Brazilian.' (Howard Wilkinson)

Kenny Dalglish: 'He may not have had great pace in his legs, but he had great pace in his head. He was very quick in his mind.' (Terry Venables)

And perhaps in contrast:

John Barnes: 'He lacked the survivors' savvy to make
   telling adjustments when the opposition sussed him out.'
   (Bertie Mee)
Vinnie Jones: 'As slow-witted in the field as a football
   donkey.' (Jeff Powell)
'He had an eternity to play the ball, but he took too long over
   it.' (Martin Tyler)
'These days I need ten minutes' notice to score.' (Joe Jordan)

Character

'We have learned that talent isn't everything. What we are doing
now is putting more time into researching the character and
temperament of a player before we sign him,' said Steve Gibson,
chairman of Middlesbrough, reflecting on the future, post-
Fabrizio Ravanelli, but pre-Paul Gascoigne. It is a delicate
operation to mesh a collection of personalities into an effective
team, as stressed by Ruud Gullit: 'I cannot emphasise enough how
important the character of a player is ... if you have too many
prima donnas, then you have no team any more.'

A range of characters and personalities can harmonise and inter-
lock within a team. Unity and individualism can co-exist only so
long as each member works for the team. Where one player
perhaps takes on the mantle of a star and sees the team as feeding
his ego, then team unity, and hence effectiveness, is demolished.
It's not the characters, but the character of the man that is important.

Perfectionist

'I want to be a perfectionist. I'm disgusted with myself if I
   give a bad ball. I feel I've failed.' (Tony Currie)
Bora Milutinovic (USA manager): 'He is a perfectionist. If
   he was married to Demi Moore, he'd expect her to be a
   good cook.' (Rick Davis, US TV summariser)

Arrogant

'I am very cocky and vain. A keeper needs charisma and
that's impossible wearing green pants.' (Sander Westerveld,
Liverpool)

'There are some bad sides to my character, but without them
I wouldn't be what I am.' (Eric Cantona)

Mischievous

Michael Hughes: 'He can be the joker in the pack – the
surprise package.' (Martin Tyler)

Paul Gascoigne: 'He would put sweets down his sock
and give them to the teacher to eat.' (Steve Stone, former
schoolmate)

Serious

Kenny Dalglish: 'He has about as much personality as a
tennis racket.' (Mick Channon)

Kenny Dalglish: 'To a degree, Kenny has marketed the dour
image to protect himself.' (Graeme Le Saux, offering a
psycho-dynamic perspective)

Impulsive

Stan Bowles: 'Impulsive, irresponsible and irreverent … he
surfed through life apparently oblivious to the height of the
waves. With him, it is not so much seize the day as grasp the
minute.' (Rob Steen)

Offbeat

Paul Gascoigne: 'He can be a loony with a fast mouth.' (John
Bailey)

Neville Southall: 'I wouldn't go so far as to say he's a
complete nut case, but he comes very close to it.' (Terry
Yorath)

Eric Cantona: 'He's a genius, but there's this other side to him. Maybe he needs someone to examine him, a psychiatrist or something.' (Chris Waddle)

'One of the trainers said to me, "Son, goalkeepers have to be crackers and daft. You, son, have got the qualities of an international." I took it as a compliment.' (John Burridge)

Ian Wright: 'The man is obviously a few sandwiches short of a picnic and it caused our club a lot of anxiety.' (Reg Burr, Millwall chairman)

'People have this perception that I'm some kind of nutcase and I'm not like that at all.' (Ian Wright)

Stan Collymore: 'I'll help Stan all I can, but I'm not going to be an amateur psychologist, nor am I going to push him around in a pram.' (John Gregory, Aston Villa)

Paul Gascoigne: 'He doesn't have a bad bone in his body but he does some stupid, ridiculous things.' (Ally McCoist)

Paul Gascoigne: 'We wouldn't have signed him if we thought he wasn't right. If he farts in front of the Queen, we get blemished.' (Adidas business manager)

Paul Gascoigne: 'There's no nastiness in him. He just might say the wrong thing or burp at the wrong time.' (Terry Venables)

Paul Gascoigne: 'Tyneside's very own Renaissance man. A man capable of breaking both leg and wind at the same time.' (Jimmy Greaves)

Paul Gascoigne: 'He makes some crazy tackles ... it's a mental problem.' (Vilfort, Brondby captain)

Vinnie Jones: 'He's just a barmpot.' (Neville Southall)

Noel Whelan: 'He's had his troubles but he has grown up a touch. There is still that barminess about him, but these days I look upon him as a harmless loony.' (Gordon Strachan)

Leadership

Those able to inspire others generate a collective effort for the cause. Leaders direct the play, carry and transmit the manager's instructions, and have the capacity to change ploy, tactics and emphasis depending on the state of the game.

Stuart Pearce: 'When you see him throw himself in front of a shot, get smacked in the face and bounce straight up, it inspires everyone else to do it.' (Steve Chettle)

Alan Hansen: 'He was a good skipper, but he could have been a really great one if he had been a bit more extrovert.' (Bob Paisley)

Tony Adams: 'He's a leader as he'll come and work behind and push people into the game.' (Bryan Robson)

Ability to dictate

'You are trying to establish a physical dominance over an opponent,' said Viv Anderson. A player may stamp his authority on a game through reputation, a quiet word in the ear of an opposing player or delivery of an early-warning bone-wobbling tackle. John Lyall was in favour of the latter: 'I slid into Peter Brabrook like an earth-moving machine with a perfectly timed challenge. From that point I was dictating the play in the little duel between us.' Referee Keith Hackett remarked on the necessity of infamy in the intimidation stakes: 'Every good side needs one iron man, but sometimes the reputation is far more fearsome than the actual article.'

Intimidation by reputation

Kenny Burns: 'It was his sheer physical presence. Frightened is not the right word to use; it was just that other teams didn't look forward to playing against him because of his reputation. You'd be surprised how important a part that plays in the game.' (Viv Anderson)

Intimidation by mouth

Vinnie Jones: 'He has a more intimidating mouth than tackle.' (Steve McMahon)

Tommy Smith: 'I would say "Come near me son and I'll break your back." It wasn't so much getting that first tackle in as the first advantage in the mind game that is part and parcel of football.'

Bill Shankly: 'Shanks used to say "Just hand them a hospital menu, son."' (Tommy Smith)

Tommy Smith: 'I played against Best and after a few shouts in his ear he used to go for a cup of tea.'

Dave MacKay: 'I was seventeen ... I was warming up near the tunnel when Tottenham came out. Dave ran out, looked across at me and shouted, "Oi Venables!". He tossed the ball over to me and said, "Have a kick now, 'cos you won't get one once the game's started." Sure enough, he was right.' (Terry Venables)

Intimidation through facials

Tommy Smith: 'You could see his expression change from disbelief that someone had whacked him to rage and one of the most threatening looks I have ever seen.' (Terry Butcher)

Paul Ince: 'A man of a thousand faces. All of them snarling.' (Jimmy Greaves)

Paul McGrath: 'He's always been an intimidating player. I used to tell him "Just look your opponents in the face, smile at them, and you'll frighten them to death."' (Jack Charlton)

Intimidation by other means

Neil Ruddock: 'It was the goading. Ruddock kept annoying Eric [Cantona] by pulling his collar down.' (Alex Ferguson)

Nobby Stiles: 'A dirty player? No, he's never hurt anyone. Mind you, he's frightened a few.' (Sir Matt Busby)

John McGrath: 'He used to threaten you before you played the match.' (Francis Lee)

Stuart Pearce: 'He can be intimidating at times, and his tackling can best be described as "ruthless".' (Steve McMahon)

Leeds United: 'You had to have eyes in the back of your head when you played against Leeds... People talk about one-touch football, but believe me, when you played them it

was down to half a touch. It was a case of getting the ball and releasing it as quickly as possible.' (Howard Kendall)
Neil Ruddock: 'He goes in for the intimidation side of the game – and I know I'm always going to get ruddy hell.' (Mark Hughes)

Chapter 7

Tactics

*'At least 50% of the game is
determined off the pitch.'*
Glenn Hoddle

A reasoned guess suggests the former England manager is referring to the analysis and exhaustive planning that are part of the preparation for a match. He may, of course, be implying that a more lofty dominion influences the outcome of a game. This is a view that may be attractive to those fans who hesitantly turn to prayer when their team desperately needs a result. However, the chalked arrows of movement on a blackboard and coloured counters in various formations on a Subbuteo pitch are more favoured by most coaches. Most modern managers are hooked on tactics. George Graham, when the boss at Arsenal, went to extreme lengths, suggesting that 'even the bulbs in my garden are in formation'.

Tactics might be considered to include planning, detailing a means of taking advantage and seeking to gain an edge over the opposition. Maybe even to confuse the opposition. Mark McGhee of Wolverhampton Wanderers appeared foxed by Birmingham City when he announced, 'Barry Fry's management style seems to be based on chaos theory.'

Tactics, of course, are only noteworthy in retrospect. Strategies and plans are made prior to the event. They rely on anticipation, both of the players carrying out the plan and of the crafty deployment of a particular system that will counter or confuse the opposition. Both can, and do, come horribly unstuck. Both Tino Asprilla, who said, 'Tactics don't really exist.

On the field it's your head that tells you what to do', and Hristo Stoichkov, who suggested, 'We need to forget about all these tactics and just play football', would perhaps not be characters whom a manager might fully entrust with an incisive or cunning plan. Critics often construe themselves as brilliant tacticians, but they generally analyse what should have been done after, not before, the event.

Some managers fly by the seats of their pants. They scoff in the face of tactical astuteness. They are also the ones that usually don't last long in their job. Barry Fry was acutely aware of his limitations in the tactics stakes. He said of Terry Venables, 'He is a great tactician, the best in the country and respected throughout the world for it, which is something I admire because I don't do tactics.'

Others, bewildered by analysis and the subtle nuances of planning, metaphorically throw their hands in the air with a sense of helplessness. 'Tactics are becoming as complicated as the chemical formula for splitting the atom,' lamented Jimmy Greaves. 'The last time I sat in front of a blackboard was at school in Scotland. It certainly never happened in all my years at Liverpool,' revealed Alan Hansen. However, for the fan accustomed to the modern game, critic and commentators alike, the challenge is to read the tactics, to fathom the manager's intent. It is a task made all the more problematic by the reluctance and inability of some players to deploy the manager's plan.

For the manager and coach, the process of developing a tactical plan revolves around five major elements.

1. Post-match analysis

Mugs of tea may be smashed against the dressing room walls, full backs lynched with sweaty jock-straps for not cutting out a cross, and the team heavily and heatedly lambasted by the manager after a sloppy defeat. This venting of emotion serves little purpose in correcting errors or influencing the approach to the next game. The reasoned manager rides the emotions and settles to an analysis of the game, perhaps a day or two later with a video of the game to replay. He takes a detached perspective. Whatever the outcome of the match – won, lost or drawn – he scans the patterns, the errors and the few occasions on which his plans worked, and notes what now needs to be done.

Some dispirited post-match reflections include:

'There was a lot of space out there but all the players abused it.' (David Pleat)

'I've just been given a video recording of the game, and I'm going to tape *Neighbours* over it.' (Harry Redknapp of West Ham, after a less than riveting 0–0 draw with Southampton)

2. Pre-match contemplation

Analysis of the opposition

An analysis of the opposing team's weaknesses and strengths may be central to how the coach trains the squad during the week prior to a game. He can then select a team that will expose the opposition's weak areas and nullify their strengths. Scouts are dispatched to check on the form of upcoming opponents, videos of games are closely dissected and dossiers on influential players are compiled. Other coaches pay no heed to the opposition and suggest that 'they should worry about us', a sentiment echoed by Barry Fry: 'I couldn't give a monkey's what the opposition do, all I worry about is what we do when we get the ball.'

'We work hard all week and they're left in no uncertain terms what the other side are good at and what I expect.' (Alan Curbishley, Charlton Athletic)

'Short of sending a couple of guys in balaclavas round with baseball bats, there's not a lot you can do to stop him.' (Hibernian manager Jim Duffy pondering on how to reduce the threat of Rangers' Brian Laudrup)

'The gaffer sent me to see if I could spot a weakness and I found one. The half-time tea's too milky.' (Kevin

Summerfield, Shrewsbury Town's coach, watching his
team's next opponents, Liverpool, demolish Leeds 5–0)
'What the scouts' reports said about Juninho frightened me
to death. So I threw 'em in the bin.' (Barry Fry, prior to his
team meeting Middlesbrough)

Playing to your strengths

If a side has a creative genius in midfield, it might seem sheer
madness to advise an approach dominated by long balls hit into
the opposing team's penalty box. As David Pleat convincingly
advocated, 'There's no advantage in any system unless it relates to
the strengths of the players at your disposal... the crux is
maximising the potential of the players you have.' This is a point
echoed by Theo Foley, who said, 'Systems are made by players
rather than players making systems', and Sir Alf Ramsey, who
suggested that 'any plan must be adapted to the strengths and
weaknesses of the players and must be acceptable to them'.
Ramsey recognised the folly of adopting a system with which
players feel unhappy.

'Be bright, make your runs, and give the ball to Juninho.'
  (Craig Hignett spills the beans on Bryan Robson's tactics)
'Our instructions were simple. Get Brian the ball, then get
  out of his road when he got it.' (Ally McCoist reveals an
  identical tactic when Brian Laudrup was in the Rangers
  line-up)
'Tactics are irrelevant when you have great players.'
  (Fabio Capello, Milan)
'I've got to say "We'll play this way" because that's best
  suited to us.' (Gordon Strachan)
'Leicester and Wimbledon play cleverly on their underdog
  status.' (Martin Tyler)
'We have to be positive otherwise we might get murdered.
  It's no good going out thinking what a great side they are
  and being in awe of them.' (John Hartson of Wales prior
  to a humiliating 7–1 drubbing by Holland)

Having the players to choose from

'We need the players, because without the players we wouldn't have a team,' suggested Howard Wilkinson perceptively. Gerard Houllier at Liverpool expanded the reasoning, saying, 'I believe in logic. If you play a system then you have to stick to it and your choice will depend on the players you have.' Squads depleted by suspensions and injuries cause managers a headache. 'When you look at our strength in depth, you'll see we have none,' grumbled Lou Macari. Reserves and juniors may be drafted in before the manger feels they are ready. Large squads of international-class players provide strength in depth, but they may also create problems. Jim Smith of Derby County noted this: 'We have strengthened in the summer, and if anything we are too strong.' Rota systems notoriously create unrest and bitterness amongst players, particularly those who appear to warm the bench more than others.

At international level the issues of tactical choice and player availability may be different. Rob Steen suggested, 'The club manager selects his tactics according to his players, the international manager his players according to his tactics.'

3. Having a game plan

'Football is as much about battles of the mind as it is battles of the boot,' said Andy Gray. An informed coach decides on a particular approach to a game and hedges his bets with an alternative in case his first tactic should fail like a squid with no suckers. Glenn Hoddle, with more than a hint of tautology, just about makes this point: 'I have a number of alternatives, and each one gives me something different.' In contrast, Mark Lawrenson noted, 'The Republic [of Ireland] have just one game plan. If plan A fails, resort to plan A.'

An effective game plan perhaps needs a more positive and detailed frame of reference than the following:

'With Northern Ireland we try to equalise before the others have scored.' (Danny Blanchflower)

'If you can't outplay the opposition, you must outnumber
   them.' (Terry Venables)
'Playing with wingers is more effective against European
   sides like Brazil than English sides like Wales.' (Ron
   Greenwood)
'If we could start scoring goals again I think that would be
   the last piece of the jigsaw.' (Liam Daish)
'The biggest thing is not to be 8–0 down after 27 minutes.'
   (Glyn Chamberlain, manager of Newcastle-under-Lyne)
'We've got Les [Ferdinand] up front, yet at times we were
   starving him. If you've got a monster up there, you must
   feed him.' (Kevin Keegan)
'I can score goals, but someone has to supply me with the ball
   first.' (Les Ferdinand: the monster shows his tactical nous)

Game plans, the beauties of which loiter in the recesses of
coaches' minds and decorate the whiteboards of every changing
room, need transmitting to players. As Andy Gray comments,
plans and tactics are 'a meeting of the minds of coaches and the
wits of the players'. Poorly developed plans and half-wits are a
recipe for disaster. Great plans succeed only when players convert
theory into action. The designer needs the material to create his
vision; players need to know their role. The players' part in the
master plan is crucial. Asking them to play out of position or in
unfamiliar roles may weaken the tapestry of the team play. Players
should feel informed about their role in the functioning of the
team. They can still lose the plot, but, as Bill Shankly said, 'It's
better to have a bad system than no system at all.'

Fans, and sometimes coaches also, construe the key roles around
the 'backbone' or central axis of the team – the goalkeeper, central
defender, midfield ball-winner and striker. The rest are somehow
considered peripheral. Yet, as Ruud Gullit suggests, 'A team is like
a clock. If you take one piece out, it doesn't work.' Perhaps the
player's position is of less importance than the role he is asked to
play. There are a number of key roles:

• At the back there might be the need for a sweeper or free
  man to cover. 'Players are able to dictate the game from the

back because that is where the space is,' said Terry Venables.

- A playmaker or midfield general. 'Playmakers will continue to be important, no matter how fast the game gets ... the guy who can pass the ball better than the rest will be important to a team strategy,' noted Croatian Robert Prosinecki.
- Defensively minded midfielders who sit deep as a shield for the defenders, play a holding role or man mark.
- Foot-soldiers who cover the wide areas, overlap or sit in front of the wing-backs. 'To be honest I'd prefer the Irish style at Leeds and less of that overlapping,' said Gary Kelly.
- Striking partners who are foils for the front man, make late runs into the box and generally covet the prized No. 10 shirt. Pelé, Cruyff, Maradona, Zico, Rodney Marsh, Tony Currie, Dennis Bergkamp, Paul Merson, Michael Owen, Paolo Di Canio and Andy Booth have all been graciously endowed with the shirt.

4. Adopting a style of play

Game plans are influenced by favoured styles. A playing style is akin to a fingerprint in reflecting the uniqueness of the manager. Some familiar styles include:

The passing game

Passing maintains possession, providing players can pass with a sense of pace and accuracy. Quick, incisive and penetrative passing is beautiful to watch and frustrating for the opposition.

'Liverpool passed it around so brilliantly early on that we had to learn to play without possession – if that doesn't sound too Irish.' (Martin O'Neill, Leicester City)
'It's not give and go, more like just give it and don't stand still.' (Jason McAteer shows he's fully conversant with the Liverpool style)

In itself, however, passing does not always win games:

'Possession and patience are myths – goals come from mistakes, not possession.' (Graham Taylor)

'I think we have got to the stage where we are passing it for passing's sake, not for the end product. In the end you can pass yourself to sleep.' (Roy Evans, Liverpool)

'We are taking far too many passes to go nowhere.' (Dave Bassett, Nottingham Forest)

Total or fluent football

Total football, a reliance on the versatility of all the players, was the brainchild of Ajax coach, Rinus Michels. Its philosophy stretches down to youth level, with youngsters being taught to play all positions on the park so that a striker discovers the role of a wing-back, a sweeper that of midfield creator. Total football demands that players are familiar with all the roles to enable them to switch with each other during games, cover one another, or drop deep to pull defenders out of position.

'Ajax are like an eagle, with their wings spread wide as they glide menacingly forward.' (Andy Roxburgh)

'What impresses me is that every Dutch player has a wee appreciation of every other position on the park. They spend time practising and try out the other positions so that they get to see the game from their team-mates' perspective.' (Gary McAllister)

'People keep talking about total football. All I know is about Total petrol.' (Derek Dougan)

Flair

We are seemingly locked into the benefits of one system over another. Coaches analyse in depth the benefits of four at the back, or three with two wing-backs, Christmas tree formations or five across the middle. Brazil is almost synonymous with the opposite – football played with flair and poise – although Mario Zagalo, coach of Brazil, sinisterly said, 'I would rather play ugly football and win than play attractive football and lose.' Yet some shining beacons remain:

> 'People talk about systems, but where is the system that shows you how to dribble past three defenders? That is what people come to see.' (Pelé)
> 'I'm looking forward to seeing some sexy football.' (Ruud Gullit, Chelsea)

Direct or route one football

> 'If we do play a long ball occasionally, it's a long ball. If anyone else does it, it's a wonderful pass.' (Joe Kinnear, Wimbledon)
> 'They are kicking the ball 50 yards instead of 60.' (Mike Walker on Wimbledon's change of style)
> 'If God had meant football to be played in the air, He'd have put grass in the sky.' (Brian Clough)
> 'They came at us playing direct football. They were more English than the English.' (Graham Taylor, describing how Sweden beat England in the 1992 European Championships)
> 'Instead of attempting to play the ball through them, I decided we would go over them.' (Jack Charlton, Republic of Ireland)
> 'Hump it, bump it, whack it. It might be a recipe for a good sex life, but it won't win the World Cup.' (Ken Bates)
> 'It's impossible to look any kind of player when the ball's being blasted over your head. That's the football played in Scotland.' (Paul Lambert)
> 'We like football you can watch on one television, not played so long and high that you need to stack up the TV sets to watch it.' (Alexis Dedes, manager of Greece)
> 'Everything's through the middle – they've less width than Bernard Manning.' (Mark Lawrenson)
> 'I do want to play the long ball and I do want to play the short ball. I think long and short balls is what football is all about.' (Bobby Robson)

Attacking style

'What's the point of going out to defend when we have so many
creative players here.' (Kevin Keegan, Newcastle United)
'It was hara-kiri at times, but we are still in the driving seat.'
(Kevin Keegan, reflecting on Newcastle's brave policy)
'As for negative and positive play, I thought that was
something for the club electrician.' (Bob Paisley)

Defensive

Ruud Gullit, taking over at Newcastle, asked, 'How can you ever
attack unless you have a solid base?' He was keen to create a
balance, a desire shared by Colin Todd of Bolton Wanderers,
whose philosophy is 'good teams are built on clean sheets'. This is
different from tactical plans that emphasise defence, such as when
teams set their stall out by pitching in their own half, back-
pedalling for their lives or sitting back with intent to spoil,
intimidate or seek damage limitation.

'There's always danger when you face a team that puts an
emphasis on defence.' (Craig Brown prepares Scotland for
Estonia)
'We shall be as positive as we can, and look to pick up a
point.' (Bobby Robson)
'I have told the team that if we don't give away a goal, we
don't lose.' (Terry Venables)
'Some teams are so negative they could be sponsored by
Kodak.' (Tommy Docherty)
'I know I may come over as a miserable git, but that was
kamikaze football. Great for the fans, but nobody will win
the Championship with defending like that.' (Roy Evans
after Liverpool beat Newcastle 4–3)
'It's easy to beat Brazil. You just stop them getting 20 yards
from your goal.' (Bobby Charlton)
'Our defending was diabolical. I need someone big and ugly
at the back who doesn't mind getting his nose broke.' (Terry
Westley)

'They are obviously having serious trouble with Bohemians' four-man back four.' (Eamonn Gregg, Irish TV analyst)

'We ground out a result. We're a grinding team from a working class area.' (Lou Macari, Stoke City manager)

'It's a great satisfaction to see two teams I coached draw 0–0.' (George Graham as Tottenham Hotspur draw with Arsenal)

'We always forget to shut the back door.' (David Jones, Southampton)

5. Changing tactics during the game

Making alterations from the touch-line is hazardous at best. Top players, according to Gerard Houllier, should be able to change tactics as the game develops: 'At international level your players should be tactically aware. They must be flexible, according to the way the opposition are playing.' A change of pace or tempo is a typical way in which some players can influence the game. Gary McAllister was one such influential player, described by Dennis Bergkamp as 'the metronome – he makes them play quicker or slower'.

John Greig on the other hand is less sure of the power to control the pace of a game: 'Football is not like an electric light. You can't just flick the button and change from slow to quick.' Whether light can ever be slow is a moot point, but modern football is generally regarded as played at full speed. From the first whistle the game is flat out: players are on full throttle and firing on all cylinders. 'I love the speed of the game here. Playing from goal to goal, keeping the momentum going at all times. There's beauty in the game here. The spontaneity is beautiful,' said Eric Cantona, supporting the notion of pace in British football.

Sometimes when games are comfortably won players coast, take the foot off the gas or loaf on the pedal. Maintaining the motoring metaphor, Ruud Gullit, however, believes it is possible to dictate the tempo during a game: 'Football is like a car. You've got five gears and the trouble with England teams is that they drive all the time in fourth or fifth. They never use first, second and third. Never build up as they should.'

Few managers seem comfortable with the notion that players will make the correct adjustments. They rarely leave a tactical switch to the players, and most are on their feet bellowing orders from the first minute. A manager agitatedly shows a set of fingers to the captain. Does he mean five across midfield, five minutes to go, pick up their number five or we need a hat-full of away goals to win on aggregate?

Breaks in play provide an opportunity to alter things, to take control. The seasoned pro may create a distraction or force a break if under pressure. An injury is a convenient way to end a spell of pressure and disrupt the opposition's momentum. A goal is a vulnerable time, the break and celebrations causing a distraction from the task in hand. Ron Atkinson, when he was at Sheffield Wednesday, provided a flavour of this when he reflected, 'I was truly elated for fifteen seconds. We were still watching the action replay when they equalised.' Other vulnerable times, when the better coach might seek to take an advantage, are when attacks break down, allowing a fleet-footed side to counter-attack with venom. Sir Alf Ramsey made this point: 'A team is most vulnerable when it has just failed in attack.' Furthermore, like the wounded tiger, a side can be at their most threatening when they survive a bombardment from the opposition. They assume control by virtue of survival. Tony Gubba, the commentator, agreed, suggesting that, 'So often the pendulum continues to swing with the side that has just pulled themselves out of a hole.'

Half-time is the longest break. Time to rethink. In many respects, it is the team on top that does not want the break. 'It's a shame half-time came as early as it did,' lamented Gordon Durie. After 45 minutes you'd imagine. But psychologically, if a team is on top, having all the pressure, half-time is not a good time. It breaks the momentum.

The manager can wield a massive influence through substitutions. Warming up the benchwarmers can motivate those who may feel a threat of being brought off. Throwing on a fresh pair of legs can generate renewed effort, add force to the attack or change the method of play. At the very least, it causes a break. Sometimes, frustratingly for the neutral, substitutions are made to waste time at the end of a game.

'England have three fresh men: three fresh legs.' (Jimmy Hill)

'He still has a fresh pair of legs up his sleeve.' (John Greig)

'Duncan McKenzie is like a beautiful motor car. Six owners and been in the garage most of his life.' (John Toshack)

'Merson throws a wobbly after being taken off at Leicester. Tough shit. I don't give a toss. I've got to do what's best for the team.' (John Gregory, Aston Villa)

Chapter 8

Discovery

*'Waddle's shot on to the bar was a marvellous
effort, something you can't teach anyone to do.'*
David Pleat

This quote poses a number of questions. Firstly, would any coach
want to tutor the art of crashing a ball against the crossbar, no
matter how electrifying the event during the course of a match?
The target undoubtedly should be the net, not the woodwork.
Secondly, is there only a select band of players – the Chris Waddles
of this world – to whom a coach might attempt to teach the most
intricate and complicated skills? This denies the donkeys, those
perceived to be less gifted, an opportunity to acquire sublime
techniques. Yet we all have the capacity to learn the new. Whether
we do engage in the process is often more to do with an attitude of
preparedness than learning potential (on which more will be said
later). Finally, the quote raises the distinct possibility that some
skills are just too difficult to teach. Players acquire them by
osmosis, accidentally or because of their genetic endowment. This
is both fatalistic and pessimistic. It implies that attempts to teach
some skills are futile. We might just as well let nature take its
course and spend our time in more worthwhile activities, such as
reading the daily paper.

Learning is the process by which we acquire new skills. As
infants we start as ill-coordinated incompetents with a tendency
to pick the ball up rather than kick it. (Some might feel the back-
pass rule has brought to light those still stuck in this elementary
stage of development, namely those goalkeepers who remain
inclined to pick up the ball.) The world is unfamiliar and uncertain at first. Footballs do damn strange things, such as bounce,

come at you at head height and fail to go in the intended direction once kicked.

Acquiring mastery over the ball takes hours of practice, anticipating the spin and pace, judging the point at which to control the ball, co-ordinating body position in relation to the ball and striking it with perfect timing. We become experimenters, trying out new ways of hitting a volley or trapping a chest-high rocket. The ball and its behaviour become less uncertain. Our actions in relation to the ball become more subtly construed. We may even come to think of ourselves as half-decent footballers. In this way learning might be understood as the ability to convert strangeness into known-ness. What was perplexing becomes familiar. Yet high crosses still cause goalkeepers to flap, and strikers continue to misdirect headers in front of an open net. For some players the ball still appears to remain a mystery.

Mastering the basics is fundamental and assumed to be a requisite for playing at any level, a point well elaborated by Brian Clough when he said, 'Coaching is for kids. If a player can't trap a ball and pass it by the time he's in the team, he shouldn't be there in the first place. I told Roy McFarland to go out and get his bloody hair cut – that's coaching at top level.'

Coaching is often considered to be the means by which players acquire the necessary skills. The enthusiasm and passion of coaches foster a desire to improve. Coaches provide the climate for learning, not what is learnt. It is the player who grapples with the new and unknown. It is the player who seeks to make sense and adjust his actions and technique in searching to improve. Coaches teach, but players learn. 'Shankly was idealistic. He wanted perfection. He wasn't a coach. He wasn't a tactician. He was an enthusiast and a teacher. He preached simplicity. Pass it and move,' observed Roy Evans.

The best coaching relies on an understanding of the player's perspective. It is adapted and tailored to suit each player's needs. Coaching that lacks this sense of understanding becomes dull and routine, and players switch off and go through the motions. Tony Dorigo hints at this when describing his experience at Leeds United under Howard Wilkinson: 'It's repetitive stuff, some of it, but it does sink in eventually.'

There are certain things that coaches should understand about each player, and thus about their capacity to take on board what is being taught:

The favoured modality

The way in which players are taught should reflect the way in which they learn most effectively. Their receptiveness to new information will depend on how it is presented to them. Some players respond better to verbal instructions, others to visual information.

Verbal messages require players to listen, decipher the meaning and convert the intention into action:

'We're not too fond of coaching. Coaxing is a better word.' (Bill Shankly)

'Sometimes a manager will say something and you'll think: "Well, I don't know about that." But with Terry [Venables] you think "Yeah!" Whenever I go back to him now, I learn something.' (Darren Anderton)

'Richard Shaw has a brain like a sponge ... he remembers everything you tell him.' (Alex Miller)

'It's just hard work and confidence. Most of this coaching talk is a load of cobblers.' (Joe Kinnear)

Visual information requires players to observe how the skill is done and attempt to mimic or make a carbon copy. Captains set examples, coaches demonstrate techniques, the masters give an object lesson. Some players even strive to act as if they are the person on whom they are seeking to model themselves.

'Shankly was a model; a man to look up to.' (Tom Finney)

'I met Maradona. It was a flash of lightning. I don't think anyone like Diego will ever be born again. I've learnt so much just from watching him.' (Gianfranco Zola)

'I once saw Alan Ball trap the ball with his backside and I thought, "If he can do that, so can I," so I went out and did it.' (George Best)

'If young players don't learn from Peter [Beardsley], they have got to be thick.' (Kevin Keegan, Newcastle United)

'I like to watch Gareth Southgate play, watch the positions he takes up and the way he handles different players.' (Gareth Barry)

'In this game you learn by example. The players are becoming better because of Ruud Gullit.' (Glenn Hoddle, Chelsea)

'Wolves keeper John Burridge has consciously modelled himself on the great Peter Shilton … same sort of hairstyle.' (Bryon Butler)

'Ron Atkinson's still a child at heart. In training this season he's been everyone from Arnold Muhren to David Ginola.' (Gordon Strachan)

'I was doing a Schmeichel – when you make a save, jump to your feet and bellow at defenders; it gives the impression you know exactly what you are talking about.' (Chris Day)

The capacity for analysis

The more thoughtful player will reflect on a game, particularly his own contribution and performance, using the opportunity to assess his shortcomings and failings, and seek to find ways of addressing the weakness. Ray Wilkins suggested, 'Generally speaking, players don't analyse themselves and their game enough … An individual knows what's wrong with his game, knows what's required to put it right. He shouldn't need telling to go out and improve his weak foot or make his first touch better.'

'Once upon a time he [Alan Hudson] would go to bed after a game and replay it in his head, re-living, correcting, observing.' (Rob Steen)

'I see everything that happens as an opportunity to learn.' (Damien Duff, Blackburn Rovers)

'I woke up thinking about games, replaying moments. I would check out my position in my mind when a goal had been scored against us, constantly thinking about how I could do better.' (Tony Adams)

'The highs are easy, the lows are for learning.' (Tony Adams)

'I learned from experience, of course. I learned to release the ball to a player in a better position and then run through, making space for the return.' (George Best)

'If I've learned anything, I've learned not to sign any more Romanians.' (Harry Redknapp after his experience with Radicioiu)

'We were complaining to the referee at the time Maradona took the free kick. But we're learning fast – next time, we'll hold the ball while we talk.' (Rashidi Yekini, Nigeria)

'While I was out I learnt a lot of things. I learnt that in a football career you can't have only highlights.' (Marc Overmars)

'Vinnie Jones has now been sent off 11 times, the record of a thug … he is certainly not learning with the passage of time. In other words he hasn't got a footballing brain.' (Ken Rogers)

'Steve Nichol was the best two-footed player in the game, but not exactly a deep thinker.' (Mark Lawrenson)

Dedication

The desire to better oneself through practice, usually with an emphasis on quality rather than quantity, marks out a top player. Such players make training and practice count. They use the moment productively. They are not interested in massed repetition, but grooving a technique to perfection.

'[Kenny] Dalglish returned to Parkhead every afternoon to practise his ball skills.' (Billy McNeill, Celtic)

'I started practising kicking the ball against the crossbar [to avoid having to keep fishing the ball out of the net, when he practised shooting on his own]. From the penalty spot, then from 20 yards, then from 30, then from 40. After I had mastered that I started working on my weaker left foot.' (George Best)

'When I was teaching myself I would set myself little tasks like kicking the ball from 40 yards with just the right weight

on it so that it stopped within 6 inches of the corner flag.'
(George Best)

'I wish I'd been as dedicated at 24 as I am now. I'd have
trained more, kept out of McDonald's, got some early
nights.' (John Barnes)

'When Ray Wilson and Denis Law played each other in
training, it was worth ten bob to watch it because they had
ability, dedication, guts and ambition. A world-class player
is one who does everything he should do.' (Bill Shankly in
his days managing Huddersfield)

'I love football ... even when I went to bed with my wife I was
training.' (Diego Maradona)

'I hate training. I hate running, but at Liverpool they say if
you don't put it in at training, how do you expect to put it in
during a match?' (Robby Fowler)

Keeping an open mind

Alert and enthusiastic players have enquiring minds. They have a
willingness to try out new things, such as mental rehearsal or
visualisation.

'The night before a match I would lie in bed and plot what I
was going to do on the field next day. I used to imagine
myself pushing the ball between the legs of the defender
who I knew would be marking me; and the next day I
would go out and do it.' (George Best)

'Our methods are so easy, sometimes players don't understand them at first.' (Joe Fagan, Liverpool)

'My mind is very, very open and so is my mouth.' (Tony
Banks, MP, former Minister of Sport)

The capacity to generalise

Taking what is learnt on the training pitch and staging it in the
match is the ultimate. The near-post corners, set pieces around the
box and crosses from deep that are practised on the training pitch
require players with a strength of character to try them out during

a match. Many players, in contrast, revert to type under pressure, avoid the new and go back to what they are familiar with.

> 'We looked bright all week in training but the problem
> with football is that Saturday always comes along.'
> (Keith Burkinshaw)
> 'Under pressure, the last thing you learn is the first thing you
> forget.' (Terry Venables)

Meeting the needs of the self

Practice and technique development improve a player's skill. Experiences change a player's character. This was emphasised by Fabrizio Ravanelli when he said, 'I am growing as a person through the English experience. Defeat builds character.' Improvement brings about change in us. A philosophical issue raised by change, however, hinges on the question of whether we are indeed the same person, if we have made changes. Most individuals have a sense of stability over time, even though they sometimes make dramatic changes to their lives and themselves. We carry our sense of self and uniqueness with us, irrespective of how we improve or change. There is fundamentally a stability in how we perceive ourselves.

Interestingly, our view of ourselves can limit progress. By construing ourselves in a particular way, we may resist acting in a certain way because it would challenge our sense of self. If a player considers himself weak on the left foot, he may be tempted to avoid shooting with this foot because it fits with his view of self. Players can fear change which threatens a self-perception. This may explain why players find it difficult to adjust, play a new role or adapt under pressure. 'I know I've got problems with my temper but I just can't change ... I will learn from experience because I am still very young,' said Julian Dicks, substantiating the point that it is not experience itself which changes people but the meaning they attach to the experience. Dicks didn't change because it was important for him to play the game his particular way – with passion, his heart on his sleeve, reacting to perceived injustices in the only way he was prepared to entertain.

Some players just feel there is nothing else to learn. 'Nothing will ever make me wiser, and there's nothing I need to be wiser about,' said Eric Cantona.

Chapter 9

Ambitions

'True motivation comes from within yourself.'
Glenn Hoddle

Someone fully engaged and committed to a task rarely thinks of motivation. They have purposes and expectations, desires and a wish to change, but not motives. Motivation is an onlooker's perspective. As such, the contrast – a lack of motivation – becomes a convenient explanation for a coach or manager to give following a less than commendable performance. Perhaps not in public, but a manager will dress down players in the changing room, with a motivational frame of reference. A lack of effort, complacency and half-heartedness, interspersed with the odd expletive, are familiar criticisms levelled at players. What sense this makes to any player is debatable, given that it is a rare event for a player to construe a bad performance in terms of poor motivation.

'In life, you have people who are motivated forever and those who are never motivated for anything. The more I work with people, the more I think this is true,' stated Arsenal manager Arsène Wenger. Whether this is a truism or not, it is possible to consider that people act in ways that validate their view of themselves. If players construe themselves as winners, it is likely they will strive as best they can to behave as winners – to compete and fully immerse themselves in the demands of the task. Only by acting in such ways can they maintain their view of themselves as winners. To perform with less than 100% commitment exposes such a player to threat. It raises the possibility that their self-evaluation is faulty, such that they cannot fully consider themselves winners if they fail to compete.

Such a perspective implies that winners are essentially competing against themselves. They seek to elaborate some aspect of themselves. The opposition are, of course, important, but as a backdrop, upon which the individual tests himself in pursuit of self-validation. Ron Atkinson describes Bryan Robson's reaction to a roasting: 'I had insulted him and he had shown me in return what he was all about. He guarded that reputation of his very jealously. Like all great players, he believed nobody had the right to question him. Or else. In that vengeful mood Robson was more lethal than a wounded lion. And psychologically I used the trick to wind him up.'

The active elaboration of self is the motivational spark. We seek to confirm our view of ourselves. The pursuit of this is often described in terms of passion or aggression. 'Aggression is fine in football, provided it is channelled in the right direction,' suggested Larry Lloyd. Competitive individuals compete. They compete because in this way they discover more about themselves. At the very least, they confirm to themselves their competitive spirit or edge. Tommy Smith confirmed this in his excuse for clattering a radio broadcaster during a charity match: 'I was an international player because I'm competitive and I don't have a choice … it's my nature. That's what I do. You're on the ball and I want you off it.'

Those competitive selves:

Julian Dicks: 'His aggression and lack of respect for anybody
  on the opposition showed at a very early stage.' (Steve
  Whitton)
Neil Ruddock: 'I always make sure Neil's on my side in train-
  ing. There's not an ounce of compromise in him.' (Ian
  Rush)
Gordon Strachan: 'Good game or bad, the bottom line was
  that he always wanted the ball. Exactly the mental courage
  I appreciate.' (Alex Ferguson)
Tommy Docherty: 'He was like a juggernaut behind me
  in the team. He was a relentless competitor throughout
  a game.' (Tom Finney)
Steffen Freund: 'To win the game you have to play with
  power and with passion and this is how I play.'

Alan Hansen: 'If I play my son at snooker, I want to
    thrash him.'
Peter Schmeichel: 'I hate losing. It stinks.'
Chris Sutton: 'I hate losing and I don't tend to speak much
    after a defeat. Footballers must be murder to live with –
    every one I know is grumpy.'
Kevin Keegan: 'He's desperate to win every time,
    whether it's the FA Cup Final or a game of head tennis.'
    (Brian Kilcline)
Norman Hunter: 'His attitude was quite daunting – it was as
    if he regarded being beaten as a personal affront, something
    to be later rectified.' (Trevor Brooking)
Dave MacKay: 'The cornerstone: a competitor at every level
    who lost his temper with himself and his team-mates
    whenever we lost.' (Brian Clough)
Dave MacKay: 'He had a die hard, desperate will to win.'
    (Emlyn Hughes)
Alex Ferguson: 'He wants to be a winner and he wants
    to be associated with winners and if you don't match
    that then you don't get on. It's as simple as that.'
    (Steve Bruce)

Those who perhaps lack the competitive edge might also
strangely be described as aggressive in the sense of elaborating
themselves. They are actively pursuing some other aspect of
themselves – perhaps being cultured, creative or cool.
Unfortunately, their lack of desperation in the will to win stakes
makes them targets for accusations of laziness, loafing, hiding or
going missing.

Those accused:

Trevor Brooking: 'He floats like a butterfly, and stings like
    one.' (Brian Clough)
Jason Euell: 'He's injured because he was only half
    committed to it.' (Andy Gray)
Cyrille Regis: 'With just a little of the competitive chemistry
    of, say, a Denis Law, he would have been terrifying, the
    complete master.' (Ron Atkinson)

Gica Popescu: 'He's a bloody moaner. If he had a cracked
  eyelash he wouldn't want to play.' (Alan Sugar)

Motivation is the rallying call. It relies on sparking the desire to
compete. Francisco Gento said of team-mate Alfredo di Stefano,
'Most of all he would make us want to win.' The effect of one
leader, one man determined to compete, rubs off on others; like
the pebble in the river, the ripples invade all. 'From the moment
Ajax's players ran on to the pitch you could see they knew they
were going to win,' noted Artur Jorge. In contrast, the opposite
state, one of complacency, can equally infect team members.
'Their attitude was that they wanted to be winners. Ours was to be
prima donnas,' explained John Sillett of Coventry City as they lost
to Northampton Town in 1990.

Managers and coaches who understand the players' perspective
tend to draw the best from them. Brian Clough said, 'I couldn't
motivate a bee to sting you if it didn't have the equipment. I
couldn't motivate a snake to bite you if it didn't have any teeth.
You can only bring out of people what they are capable of giving.'
Clough was spot on. Employing his favoured animal metaphors,
the former Nottingham Forest manager highlighted the importance of understanding each player's personal desire. Good
managers discover how the game can elaborate a player's notion
of himself. They channel that individual pursuit.

Motivation is often implied through metaphor, with a broad
range of candidates.

Desire

As in pursuit of sexual gratification, players are variedly
described, prior to a match, as up for it, wanting it or fancying it.
'Some players you can whip, some players you can tickle,' said
Ron Atkinson, elaborating (perhaps unwittingly) on the theme.

Heart

'You play this game with your hearts.' (John King, Tranmere
  Rovers)

'Mark Hughes played his heart out – a performer to stir the
  soul of any red-blooded supporter.' (Ron Atkinson)
Bryan Robson: 'There has never been a better player with
  such a combination of ability and heart in the history of
  our business.' (Ron Atkinson)
Chris Sutton: 'That's a good deal for Blackburn because he's
  got a heart as big as his new wage packet.' (Ian Butterworth)
'It's hard to be passionate twice a week.' (George Graham of
  Arsenal bemoaning the demanding schedule of games)
'Their hearts weren't in it because they're a bunch of
  pansies.' (Brian Clough, Nottingham Forest)

The battle cry

Battling for every ball; playing as if your life depended on it;
digging in; fighting for the cause; pulling no punches; and killing
off the challenge. All these suitably reflect the war-like nature of
competition.

'Football is like war. When the chips are down, you need
  fighters.' (Ian Branfoot, Southampton)
'When I ask for one more charge they put the tin hats on
  and go over the top again.' (Joe Kinnear, Wimbledon)
'Managers want players who are going to put their life on
  the line for him. If you were at the bottom of the league
  struggling, would you call on Gary Lineker?' (Vinnie Jones)
'I play every game to win. I go out to die for my team.'
  (Vinnie Jones)
'If I sense that any player of mine is not psyched up and
  giving absolutely everything, I'll put a bullet in the back of
  his neck.' (Johan Cruyff, Barcelona)
'Get your tin helmets out.' (Dave Bassett of Sheffield United,
  preparing to meet Leeds United)
'Mark Hughes is a warrior you could trust with your life.'
  (Alex Ferguson)
'I am very combative on the pitch.' (Mark Hughes)
'There will be no war painting the dressing room.'
  (Craig Brown, Scottish manager, settling the troops)

'We didn't go to war. We didn't even get the bullets out – we fired blanks all day.' (John King, Tranmere Rovers, after losing 5–0 at Derby County)

Hunger

The alimentary canal provides an interesting source of motivational expressions. Players may have that extra bite, have the stomach to fight for the cause or the guts to take on a formidable opponent. The very same passageway, in its nether regions, also provides an expression or two to depict a lack of motivation. Players who can't be arsed provide one of the printable examples.

'The hunger has always been there. You can put up with bad performances and your touch not being right, but one thing that can never be excused is a lack of effort.' (Alan Shearer)

Bottle

'Bottle is a quality too ... It's not just about ball control and being clever. For want of a better phrase, sometimes you have to show the world what's between your legs.' (Graeme Souness)

Enthusiasm

'I left as I arrived: fired with enthusiasm.' (John McGrath, on being sacked from Preston North End)
'I don't think Vinnie Jones's football ability is of a great standard, but his enthusiasm is un-bounding.' (Tommy Smith)
'He's so enthusiastic, he's like a two year old.' (Harry Redknapp, West Ham, on his 34-year-old acquisition, Ian Wright)
'Too often players get to this stage of their careers and lose their enthusiasm. Though I must admit it's hard to get enthusiastic about a wet Monday night in Brechin.' (Charlie Nicholas giving it all for Clyde)

On fire

'I play with passion and fire. I have to accept this fire occasionally does harm. I know it does. I harm myself ... but I cannot be what I am without those other sides of my character.' (Eric Cantona)

'Nobody was igniting us. You can't light a fire without a spark.' (Kevin Keegan after England drew 0–0 with Sweden)

'He needs a rocket up his backside.' (Mark Lawrenson)

'Cyrille Regis doesn't punch his weight on the pitch. I wish I could make him push, dig and challenge a bit harder ... we are still looking to stoke up the fire.' (Bobby Robson)

The frantic urging of coaches, the vociferous advice from the terraces and the grimaced appeals from team-mates will only enhance a player's motivation if it meshes with the player's needs and pursuits. Some reasons which may invite players to raise their game, include:

A fear of failure

'People think he's just jolly old Ally, but that's not the guy I know. I know a guy who works hard and wants to score goals. He doesn't like failure.' (Jimmy Nicholl, Raith Rovers)

The challenge of something new or big

'A few weeks ago I couldn't get a team out because of injuries. On the eve of the Cup Final, I have more than 20 to choose from – it's a miracle.' (Ruud Gullit)

'I like being manager of Wimbledon. I don't think there's any challenge in being manager of AC Milan.' (Joe Kinnear)

The wet opposition

'In midwinter we'd get to some of those tough, cold grounds
in the North and we'd upset the locals by going out to play
wearing gloves. They just thought we were a bunch of
fairies. It was like a red rag to a bull with their players.'
(Bobby Moore)

Competition for places in the team

Big squads create competition. Loss of form, injury, tactical
decisions or a clash of opinion with the manager may mean a
stretch on the bench, or a run out with the stiffs. Players out of the
side ache for a chance to play. They might wish to impress the
manager with their endeavour on the training pitch or more
covertly wish the current incumbent of their place in the team to
lose form or pick up an injury. But it's not good form to express
such wishes. Players are, after all, team-mates. Goalkeepers, in
this respect, are exceptions. They tend publicly to admit they are
fighting for the No. 1 spot.

Opposition wind up or criticism in the press

Slagging off a team or a player invariably backfires. It tends to fire
them up to prove the critic wrong. To put egg on the face of an
accuser is invariably appealing. On the park Tony Adams, the
Arsenal skipper, was often greeted with 'hee-haw' donkey imita-
tions. However, he loved it and used the heckling as a source of
motivation, to prove the detractors wrong.

'Thanks to Berti Vogts for the best motivation, saying we are
only a small country. What is he going to say now when it is
3–0?' (Davor Suker, after Croatia crush Germany in the
1998 World Cup)

'They [Leeds United] raised their game because they were
playing Manchester United … it's pathetic.' (Alex Ferguson
winds up the Leeds players prior to them tackling Newcastle,
who were challenging Manchester United for the title)

'Sometimes you have to accept there's nothing you can do: extra training, psychology, getting strippers in – none of it will help.' (Dave Bassett at a low ebb at Sheffield United)

Chapter 10

Hitting the target

*'If you reach for perfection you get excellence.
If you aim for half, you don't even get that.'*
Terry Venables

As every new season dawns, expectations rise. Dreams of glory
raid the stream of consciousness. Fans and players alike eagerly
count the days to the opening match. They ache with waiting.
When the day finally arrives, fans excitedly enter the ground
through dated turnstiles, high in the hope of success. The pitch,
tantalisingly vibrant, manicured and lush, confirms a fresh start.
This season things really will be different. Programme notes
typically hint at the club's ambitions. Dishearteningly, however,
they could perhaps all be scribbled by the same public relations
outfit. To challenge for honours or promotion; to seek a place in
the play-offs; maybe a good cup run; and certainly to build on the
good work of last season. Yet only the very few grasp silverware
when May comes. 'Everybody wants to win the league, but it's
bloody hard. You can't just get out of bed and go and win it,'
reflected an erudite Sol Campbell of Tottenham Hotspur.

However, you have to haul yourself out of the sack to stand a
chance. Targets are a traditional means of publicly announcing
what the club and players are seeking to achieve. They state intent.
They aim for progress. They steer away from stagnation. As Peter
Reid of Sunderland sought to express it, 'We all know that in
football, you stand still if you go backwards.' Effective targets
are constructed along three dimensions of time, realism and
performance.

Good targets invariably have a time frame; they include a goal to
be achieved over a specified time. Clubs tend to focus on long-term

goals such as developing the youth structure, football in the community, scouting for local talent, setting up academies, putting the club back where it deserves to be and balancing the books. Although laudable, such aims are unlikely to fit with the plans of a manager who will probably not be around to reap the benefits. Clubs need long-term targets, whereas managers tend to operate over the shorter term. They have a limited life at any one club, a lesson learnt by Ossie Ardiles, who said, after being shown the door, yet again (this time by Mexican club, Guadalajara), 'Maybe I'll have to change my way of thinking. I work for the long, long term but sometimes you have to survive the short term first.'

Managers will generally have aims for the season. League games are considered the 'bread and butter' and finishing as high as possible in the league is a fundamental target. When riding high at the top, a manager often invokes caution by suggesting that only a quarter of the season has passed. When rooted at the bottom with 20 games to go, the likes of Danny Wilson at Sheffield Wednesday remind us that there are still 60 points to play for. Cup runs are distractions rather than targets for most managers. Clubs striving for league or European honours reveal their priorities through team selection and commitment during a game.

Season-long goals provide a framework within which more immediate targets may be set. Gordon Strachan, for example, shortened the time frame by considering matches in clusters. He said, 'You look at games in clumps, five or six at a time and set yourself a target for those. Then you look at the next clump and set a target for them. Otherwise you end up playing game to game.' Interestingly, the coveted 'Manager of the Month' award reinforces the notion that clusters of matches are more important than the 'next game' cliché.

However, the 'next game' is held to be paramount for most managers, even though they may not consider it a target. Unwittingly, Ron Wylie reflected the confusion over targets within targets when he stated, 'I don't really believe in targets because my next target is to beat Stoke City.' For a manager, the upcoming game means everything, even when in the overall context of the season it might mean little. Thus a mundane league match with nothing at stake, played four days before a cup semi-final, is difficult for a player to construe as a challenge, but the manager has, at least, to make noises about the importance of each game.

Some matches on the fixture list take on added importance for managers and players alike. They may become a focal point, highlighted as beacons against which to judge the whole season. Beating the champions, the current division leaders, the local rivals in a sell-out derby clash, or the club that sacked or discarded the manager acrimoniously means something extra.

Players, in contrast to managers, focus less on time frames, but modify their targets according to their career development. They may have fantasies of scoring for their country, owning some flash wheels and dating a top lap dancer, but the more immediate targets for a pimply faced trialist are to interest the youth coach, buy a Reliant Robin and walk out with the girl next door. As a blossoming career develops, a player typically sets the next target a little higher. A successful trial, the hope of a contract, a run in the reserves, the promise of a squad number, a first team debut, regular first team football, captaincy, an international honour, a transfer to a top club and a lucrative contract.

Although targets provide a sense of achievement when reached, they may appear perpetually beyond a player's grasp. Selection remains one target that is beyond a player's control, and, however good his performances might seem to be, it is the manager who makes the decision on inclusion. The press, public and club manager may proclaim a player's talent and form, but this may mean little to an international manager who has a different agenda. A player's frustration at being overlooked is exemplified by Julian Dicks of West Ham United, who said, 'I'd rather build kennels for my dogs than play for England this summer.'

Appearance and goal-scoring records emerge on the horizon as players establish themselves in a team. Most players, however, play this down in public, something that Ian Wright attempted, not entirely convincingly, by saying, 'I want the record. I'm five short – not that I'm counting', when challenging for the Arsenal all-time goal-scoring record. Brian McClair made light of a request about the number of goals he had scored for Manchester United by claiming, 'I haven't kept count. I'm not that sad a person.'

As players edge towards the end of their playing careers, they muse about putting something back into the game by becoming coaches, pundits or column writers. Others clamour for the glamour through advertisement vignettes *à la* Ginola, Clough and Lineker, hosting chat shows which are all Wright on the night, or hitting the big screen in the style of Cantona and Jones. Yet others bite the bullet and enter the world of business and commerce, selling double-glazing, newspapers or jars of ale at the local hostelry. Ally McCoist feared the prospect of retirement. He proclaimed, somewhat dramatically, 'It'll kill me when I'm no longer going out there to entertain the fans. That will be the saddest day ever. I'll have to find something else to replace that. Maybe I'll go the Richard Gere way and become a Tibetan monk and find religion.'

Realism is a second strand of target setting. Peter Beardsley appeared to share this view, but then completely baffled himself with metaphors, saying, 'Reaching the play-offs might be a bit much, but aim for the moon and you can reach the stars.' Ivano Bonetti, on signing for Grimsby Town, alluded to realism, and the importance of context, when he commented, 'There are goals to pursue here, just as there were at Juventus. They are simpler smaller goals.'

A target marks a standard. It may be realistic and thus achievable or a pipe dream. Strikers might aim to reach 20 goals in a season, a challenging target for the best Premiership strikers but beyond the grasp of most wide men, midfielders and lumbering giants leading the line. Setting the sights a little lower might see a target reached. Kenny Irons said, 'I always like to come up with a little target for myself and it's not bad if I can make it' when he moved from Tranmere Rovers, where he had scored 18 goals from midfield, to Huddersfield Town, where he set himself a target of double figures.

There is a developing realism about the Premiership, with notions of leagues within a league being alluded to. George Graham, of Tottenham Hotspur, reflected on this, when he said, 'There are three trophies in the Premiership: winning it, getting a top six place and staying up.' The Championship is often a two- or three-horse race, with seven or eight clubs striving for a top six place to achieve European qualification. Clubs in mid-table seek to maintain their position by winning home games, and the bottom four or five teams endeavour to take points from rivals for relegation in a determined dog-fight for survival.

Targets may be challenging or fail to raise any expectation. Ian Atkins reflected on the latter during his time in the North-East: 'If you think champagne you drink champagne. At Sunderland they drink water.' Realistic targets outline the possible. A perennial favourite of Martin O'Neill, at Leicester City, is to secure enough points to avoid the threat of relegation. An interesting target on the world stage was set by Rene Simoes, coach of Jamaica in France '98, when he said: 'We are the Cinderellas of the World Cup. Our mission is to postpone midnight for as long as possible.' Bob Paisley, a tough taskmaster at Liverpool, threw down the gauntlet for his successful team by musing, 'Mind, I've been here during the bad times too. One year we came second.'

Whilst targets, however quirky, have the benefit of focusing attention on what is expected, some fear the binding effect they can have. Steve Coppell refused to entertain them, but also became a slave to them when, in seeking to clarify his position, he said, 'I'm not going to make it a target, but it's something to aim for.' Gordon Strachan saw the hidden demon of targets and stated, 'I protect myself by not having too many targets.' He elaborated on this by examining the possible effects of not reaching a defined target: 'If you're obsessive and don't get to the point you want to achieve, you can become a basket case. I've seen loads of them.' Interestingly, others perceive Strachan as a taskmaster who makes high demands. Howard Wilkinson noted, 'Strachan sets standards for himself and he expects them of others. He's an achiever and achievers tend to be described as ambitious.'

Targets may therefore create pressure. Avoiding them, however, can prove difficult. It might be argued that not having targets is a target in itself. However hard some players and managers strive to avoid targets, they surface without their awareness. They are perhaps endemic to our way of life. Emile Heskey showed how targets can lurk beyond immediate awareness when he said, 'I don't set myself targets but there is always a 20 goal barrier and I know I can break it.'

The positive aspect of goals or targets is that they outline the expected outcome. They define the 'end point', the desired result, or as Stuart Pearce put it, mixing his metaphors, 'the carrot at the end of the tunnel'. For targets to be accomplished, however, effort is directed more at the day-to-day activities that will move us closer to the target. Goals are thus broken into achievable segments, and good players consider what is needed to accomplish the goal. The focus is on the here and now, not the end result.

Poor goals are platitudes. The need to win games is a classic banality. Good goals, in contrast, are about performance, not outcome, taking control over what is controllable. If a player excels when performing, the outcome will take care of itself. The result of a match is dependent on the activity of both sides (plus the officials) and thus somewhat outside the players' control. However, if players concentrate on performing to their best, taking control over their own game, then that will best influence the result. Ruud Gullit was a little ambivalent about this, saying, 'At Chelsea, we often play for the performance, not the result. That's good, but that's not what we have to aim for.' Yet the comments of both Gordon Strachan, who said, 'I can take bad games from a player, but I cannot take a dishonest one', and Kenny Dalglish, who announced, when Newcastle United manager, 'The lads can be proud of what they set out to do. Unfortunately they didn't achieve it', reflect the focus on performance rather than outcome.

Dissecting targets into individual performances means outlining each player's role and responsibility within the team effort. Tony Adams put it succinctly in saying, 'I'm in touch with what I have to do.' Good coaches identify the role and spell out clearly for each player what is expected from them in each match. Keep tight, track the runner, play it down the channel, drop deep off your marker and so forth. Concentration improves when the player knows his job and is in tune with the overall plan. Brian Clough illustrated this when he said, of himself as a player, 'I always kept my eye on the ball ... I was never, ever physically afraid. My terms of reference were basic and simple: put the ball in the net. That was my job and I allowed nothing and nobody to distract me from that purpose.'

Glenn Hoddle noted how the importance of concentration heightens as the level of competition increases: 'That's the difference at international level – the concentration has to be so high.' Conceptualising concentration in such a scaled manner is common. It is as if concentration can be measured on a thermometer, where players need to reach the zenith or peak to perform well. Neil Ruddock appears to see it this way: 'I used to dive in, take a chance and end up sliding on my backside. Now I try to judge my tackles to perfection. It calls for a different level of concentration.' Perhaps rather than construing concentration as a matter of levels, an alternative is to think of it as tuning into what is important. Rather than another level, Ruddock tuned into a different perspective – that of timing. Locking on to the importance of timing a tackle is what would improve his tackling and performance.

There is an art to maintaining concentration throughout the match, or 'being in the wide-awake club' as Ron Atkinson was fond of saying. Bobby Moore was a master: always alert, on his toes, awake to the potential threat. 'Even in the kick in I passed every ball as if the World Cup depended on it,' he said. It is not difficult to spot players who switch off, who seem unaware of danger or possibilities. They are caught napping, caught by surprise, ball watching. Half-time sometimes disrupts a player's concentration. They get caught cold with their minds still in the changing room. End of season games sometimes see players with their minds on other things, lacking commitment, as if they are already on their holidays.

Complacency can also wreck concentration. After a 1–1 draw with Southampton, Arsène Wenger of Arsenal said, 'To lose two points like that was maybe not deserved if you look at the game but maybe deserved if you were to look inside our brains. Maybe we felt it had become too easy and lost concentration at a vital moment.' Letting your mind wander has a similar effect. Tony Adams described how, with ten minutes to go in a Wembley cup final, with the score at 2–1, he 'looked up at the Royal box to where the trophy was resting, thinking that I would be lifting it in ten minutes or so'. Arsenal lost 3–2 and Adams concluded, 'I learned not to look at the prize but to concentrate on the matter in hand.' Performance counts. Focusing on what has to be done is the process of making it count.

Distractions, or potential distractions, come in many guises. The press and public are unceasing in their criticism. Tony Adams again offers a wise approach. 'No words or articles have ever affected the way I play. As far as I am concerned, the media just does not have that power over me,' he said when denying that publication of his book affected his performances for England. Poor results are another potential distraction, and Terry Venables perhaps reflects an appropriate attitude when he suggested, 'A good game is like a bad one in that you have to put it behind you as quickly as possible.'

A booking may affect a player's concentration. No longer is he focused purely on his role, as Sammy McIlroy points out: 'Once you've received a booking ... while you don't consciously think of pulling out of a tackle, you have to keep on reminding yourself that you cannot afford any more trouble, so maybe your concentration is divided between the action of the game and the knowledge that you must keep your temper.'

Intriguingly, some players and coaches feel that part of their role is to upset their opponents' concentration. The clattering neck-high tackle in the first minute gives the forward 'something else to think about'. Bursting the onion bag, yes; avoiding another jugular severing, certainly. Tommy Smith, the arch rogue and hard man of Anfield, clearly saw his job as being intimidation: 'If you can break somebody's concentration from the word go, you have immediately got an advantage,' he growled. Another Anfield legend, Bill Shankly, knew all about interfering with others' concentration. 'He was always yapping. It was generally when you were about to take a shot, he'd start yapping and put you off your stride,' said Tommy Lawton.

Ian Wright uses more subtle tricks. 'He talks the whole time, trying to wind their markers up, trying to make them lose concentration or lure them into making a foul on the edge of the box,' noted Andy Gray. Other players just have to be themselves to perplex the opposition and cause chaos. Jock Stein said of winger Jimmy Johnstone, 'Most foreign opponents have never seen anything like him before and they can lose concentration for twenty minutes trying to work him out.'

A player focused on his job delivers. His performance is what counts in terms of whether the team achieves its target. It is therefore somewhat baffling that rewards tend to accompany outcome rather than performance – trophies, medals and win bonuses are dependent on results, not performances. England, to a man, won £1,000 for winning the World Cup in 1966. Turkish forwards were offered a night with a belly dancer for scoring against Germany. Kuwaiti players were given a plot of land for qualifying for the World Cup. 'Outside of family life, there is nothing better than winning European Cups,' said Brian Clough, reinforcing the point. 'At the end of the day, it's all about what's on the shelf at the end of the year,' observed Steve Coppell, emerging from a time confusion capsule.

On the other hand, awards – players' player of the year; professional writers' player; supporters' player – tend to be judged on performance over the season, not on results. Ruud Gullit indicated the importance of performance when he suggested, 'Winning something is the dessert. The creation is the main course.' Those supporters committed to clubs that perennially struggle in the league ladder stakes may have sympathy with this sentiment.

Achieving the target is the prize. The jubilation that comes with accomplishment is an intrinsic reward. Any accompanying silverware is a bonus, as implied by Kenny Swain, Grimsby Town manager, as his side crashed at Sheffield Wednesday: 'The cup is the icing on the cake. But at the moment, we haven't got any cake.' Achieving the goal is inherently satisfying. The sense of pride, exhilaration and self-worth are colossal. It has been argued that such intrinsic rewards are the most effective way to generate a player's motivation. Some expressions of this internal satisfaction include:

'This is the most beautiful day of my life.' (Dino Zoff of Italy, holding the World Cup aloft)

'You can't buy playing for England – no money in the world can buy a white shirt.' (Alan Shearer)

'Magnifico – or whatever they say in Paris.' (Peter Reid praises his French keeper, Lionel Perez)

'For players it doesn't matter what bonus they are on,
   playing is the meat and drink and winning is the bonus. It's
   the winning that gives them the kicks.' (Alex Ferguson)
'I wouldn't give up football even if I won the £18 million
   jackpot on the National Lottery. I love this job and I'd even
   pay to play rather than not play at all.' (Dean Holdsworth)
'All I had to play for was the money and that was nothing
   compared to the feelings I get from football.' (Alan
   Hudson)

Dreams, to paraphrase the Eurythmics, are made from targets
fulfilled. Setting realistic and achievable goals moves a player
towards staggering heights of accomplishment. Michael Owen,
reflecting on progress that exceeded his expectations when he
became England's hero, said, 'I did not set myself a target to play
in the World Cup. I would never have dreamed that could
happen.' Yet, very occasionally, concentrating on the smaller
controllable targets, reaps rich rewards and wild dreams. Lawrie
McMenemy sought to make a similar point: 'Some of those
players never dreamed they'd be playing in a Cup Final – but here
they are today, fulfilling those dreams.'

Chapter 11

Excuses

'The road to ruin is paved with excuses.'
Bobby Gould

Invariably excuses are a cop-out. They perhaps lamely protect us from feeling at fault, but they ultimately limit what can be learned from an experience. The legendary squashed hedgehog might (if it could) complain about the heavy traffic, but should it have tried to cross the road before glancing in both directions? All events can be interpreted in many ways. A free kick that sails over the bar is greeted by supporters with derision, yet the player might defend himself by blaming the light ball, a wall that failed to retreat ten yards or a playing surface that was less than true. A player, in contrast, who takes responsibility might assess his technique and timing, and seek to improve swerve, dip and placement of free kicks on the practice ground.

The way in which players, coaches and managers perceive the reasons for a performance affect what they can do about it. Do they respond to a poor performance by blaming bad fortune, or perhaps alternatively examine the experience for what can be learnt? Taking responsibility means acknowledging your part in the performance, not taking the blame. It means discovering solutions so a poor performance is not repeated: working on what went wrong and altering an approach the next time. 'When you've got the jersey on, blame nobody but yourself if you fail,' warned Bill Shankly astutely.

Responsibility for a good performance should also be acknowledged and used to build confidence and consistency. 'The best team always wins. The rest is only gossip,' said Jimmy Sirrel of Notts County. 'We beat them five nothing and they were lucky to score nothing,' said Bill Shankly in typical style. In contrast, little is gained by attributing success to factors beyond our control, as when Hristo Stoichkov asserted 'God is a Bulgarian' after a penalty shoot-out victory over Mexico in 1994. Or when Claudio Taffarel of Brazil, after another successful penalty shoot-out against Holland in 1998, claimed, 'It wasn't me making those saves, it was God.'

Those who take responsibility for their own performance have the opportunity to improve and enhance their future performances. When Kenny Dalglish said, 'We have to look at ourselves for the reasons we lost', it demonstrated his grasp of this principle. Similarly Joe Royle, manager of Everton, was willing to examine his own part in another defeat when he said, 'I don't blame individuals. I blame myself', although it remains an open question as to whether he regarded himself as an individual. Roy Evans at Liverpool recognised that the usual platitudes were insufficient for one particular defeat: 'I'd like to go through all the usual clichés, only it was worse than that.' On occasion, it may not be possible to identify the cause, but at least Joe Royle was not prepared to make an excuse when he admitted, 'I haven't got a clue why we played like that', as Everton lost to York City.

Making excuses through blaming others or the conditions externalises the problem. It absolves oneself from responsibility, and as such, little can be done to rectify the problem. 'Players hide behind every excuse in the book – they aren't facing up to their responsibilities,' observed a discerning Alan Ball. Issues are conveniently swept under the carpet, but they remain there to surface at some future embarrassing moment. Peter Reid showed a realisation of this principle in reflecting, 'I don't think we deserved to lose 3–0, but I keep saying that.'

And some bizarre, obscure and mind-boggling excuses have arisen in a desperate attempt to avoid taking responsibility. Glenn Hoddle blamed the absence of his guru, Eileen Drewery, for England's early exit from France '98. (As an aside, Neil Webb curiously suggested that Eileen 'gives players a shoulder to talk to'.) Ron Saunders blamed Birmingham City's run of bad luck (which incidentally stretches back a century or more) on a curse laid by gypsies following their eviction from the ground. A neat try. Here are a few more corkers:

'Nobby clipped him from behind. Out came my book and Stiles, full of apologies, pleaded, "It's the floodlights, ref. They shine in my contact lenses and I can't see a thing."' (Referee Pat Partridge)

'I never touched him. I don't know why he fell on the ground – perhaps it was my after-shave.' (Ricky Otto)

'The grass was too long.' Christian Gross after Spurs go down the Swanee at Wimbledon)

Shirt design: Alex Ferguson blamed a grey away strip for Manchester United being trounced at the Dell: 'It was really a matter of vision. Our players said it was difficult to see their team-mates at distances when they lifted their heads.'

'Something as trivial as a change of month can sometimes make the difference. I hope it does the trick for us because I'm certainly glad to see the back of October.' (Brian Little, Stoke City)

'We played them on the wrong day.' (Graham Taylor, after England lost to the USA in 1993)

'I now realise that computer games have affected my performance badly.' (David James of Liverpool, blaming digital over-activity for his suspect ball-handling)

Beware those who imply that 'external factors' are a reason for either success or failure. Usually a player, coach or manager is only too willing to credit themselves with success, putting it down to their efforts. Occasionally, however, managers just don't grasp it. When asked why Watford were on a good run of results, manager Glen Roeder said, 'The secret? I'm not sure. If I knew, I would can it and sell it.' In contrast, failure is feverishly put down to factors over which the coach or manger has no control, which limits what can be learnt and put right for the next performance.

Sifted from the myriad possible excuses, the well-worn avenues of blame include:

Bad luck

'We were desperately unlucky to lose those last four games.'
(Terry Dolan, Hull City)

'We didn't have the run of the mill.' (Glenn Hoddle)

'I'm not a believer in luck, although I do believe you need it.'
(Alan Ball)

'The only thing I wish is that when I come back on this earth I
will be born lucky, instead of talented.' (Bobby Campbell)

'Sometimes the best team doesn't win.' (Craig Brown before
Scotland play Sweden, hoping for divine intervention)

'Right now if I robbed a bank, I'd get mugged on the way
out.' (Brian Horton, Manchester City)

'We have been unlucky with the way fixtures have fallen; that
so many away matches have followed European games.'
(Alex Ferguson of Manchester United, seeking maybe to
influence the fixture list)

'The worst thing that could have happened to us was for
their keeper to break his arm.' (Alan Buckley, West
Bromwich Albion manager, after yet another defeat)

'Penalty shoot-outs have nothing to do with football. It's like
shooting poor wee ducks at a fair ground.' (Alex Smith,
Aberdeen)

'With our luck, one of our players must be bonking a witch.'
(Ken Brown, Norwich City)

'I look at myself every night and wonder if, perhaps, I've run
over a black cat or knocked down a nun.' (David Jones,
Southampton manager, after yet another disastrous start to
a season)

'I must have broken a job lot of mirrors and run over a few
black cats.' (Mike Walker, Everton)

Barry Fry sees the light and changes his opinion about class and
luck. He remarked, 'The first time I saw Le Tissier I thought,
"Lucky bastard, he's chipped that pass 80 yards." After the fourth
time, I thought, "Maybe he's not so lucky after all."' In a similar
vein, Gordon Strachan put forward a reasoned argument, one that
enables something to be done about the problem, saying, 'It

wasn't so much a case of bad luck, as bad finishing.' Craig Brown, Scotland coach, makes a similar point in stressing, 'They wouldn't have been able to score a "lucky" goal if they hadn't been in our six yard box', when Brazil scored against them.

Blaming other players

'Peter Barnes had an abundance of skill but no strength of mind ... He would always blame others, repeatedly offering the lamest excuse for his own shortcomings.' (Ron Atkinson)

'I made a mistake [pushing over the referee] but others are guilty as well as me.' (Paolo Di Canio)

'Andy [Cole] should be hitting the target from those distances, but I'm not going to single anyone out.' (Alex Ferguson)

'Le Tissier is the most talented footballer in Britain but if he is honest with himself he knows he could do a lot more than he did last season.' (Graeme Souness)

'If you had to name one particular person to blame it would have to be the players.' (Theo Foley)

'The two players concerned, Craig Burley and Gordon Durie, were sleeping a bit.' (Craig Brown points a finger or two at his players as Scotland go a goal down to Brazil)

'Without being too harsh on David Beckham, he cost us the match.' (Ian Wright on England's exit from the 1998 World Cup)

Blaming the manager

(This route is rarely risked by a player.)

'One thing I've learned since becoming a manager is that in the public's mind, players win games and managers lose them.' (Bryan Robson)

'The manager gets too much credit when things go well and too much blame when they don't.' (Graham Taylor, Watford)

'They will either plant kisses on my bald pate or throw
  tomatoes at it.' (Arrigo Sacchi, manager of Italy, after his
  team bow out of Euro '96)

Blaming the pitch

Alex Ferguson complained about the state of his own club's
'Theatre of Dreams' pitch, claiming it was responsible for his
team's lack-lustre performances against Newcastle United and
Blackburn Rovers.

'Highfield Road has more divots than Gleneagles.' (Glenn
  Hoddle)
'I didn't think the pitch was fit to play on, but I wouldn't use
  that as any kind of excuse.' (Alan Buckley, striving to make
  sense of yet another defeat)

Howard Wilkinson took a more enlightened view, suggesting,
'It's the best pitch they will play on today', as England prepared to
meet Bulgaria on a pitch littered with flint and glass in the
goalmouth.

Blaming inclement weather

'Any more snow and I'll need a periscope.' (Gianfranco
  Zola, the diminutive one, as Chelsea travel to the frozen
  north to face Tromso in a blizzard)
'It got a bit chilly here after Christmas, mind. There was
  even a bit of frost on the ground at training one day.'
  (John Collins, tongue in cheek, on life in Monaco)
'The heat was a great leveller.' (Chris Waddle, Burnley
  manager, putting a poor performance down to the deserts
  of the North-West)
'Hopefully we can keep the rain going all season.' (Tommy Taylor
  of Leyton Orient, after two wins in a week on mud baths)
'You wouldn't fight a war in those sort of conditions.'
  (Howard Wilkinson of Leeds United, as they prepare to
  do battle with Barnsley in the wind)

A refusal to credit the opposition

'There was nothing between the teams apart from seven
   goals.' (Danny Wilson, seeing equity as Barnsley crash at
   Manchester United)
'Coventry in all honesty never really looked like scoring.'
   (Alex Ferguson, typically devaluing the Sky Blues as they
   beat Manchester United 3–2)

Blaming the officials

The plea that most easily slips off the tongue is blame for the
referee, apparently the easiest of targets. What is rarely considered
is how one can accuse bias in another (such as a referee) when the
accuser is biased. Perhaps a tad philosophical, but all managers
and coaches perceive events through team-coloured spectacles. A
few examples:

'The official today was a muppet.' (Ian Wright)
'In all fairness the referee had a complete cerebral failure.'
   (Rick Holden)
'This is the fifth time this season we've finished up with ten
   men, and I think it is about time the Referee's Association
   had a look at it.' (Joe Kinnear, neatly externalising
   Wimbledon's disciplinary record)
'I have to hand it to Manchester United. They have the best
   players – and the best referees.' (Sam Hammam)
'I think the referee took a wee bit of gloss off Newcastle's
   performance … we'll just put it down as a blip and get on
   with it.' (Alex Ferguson, putting a 5–0 thrashing down to
   referee error)
'We just didn't get any crucial decisions.' (Alex Ferguson,
   attributing the 6–3 thrashing by Southampton to the
   referee)
'My certain feeling is of being raped week in, week out
   by referees and linesmen, and it just cannot go on.' (Sam
   Hammam)

'Referees take from the small clubs and give to the big boys.
The facts of life are that the dice is loaded against the
poorer people.' (Sam Hammam)

'I've seen referees who aren't fit to officiate on Copacabana
beach.' (Gerson)

'Some of the decisions we have been getting lately are so
bizarre they are bordering on the Twilight Zone.'
(Sam Hammam)

'Can anyone tell me why they give referees a watch? It
certainly isn't to keep the time.' (Alex Ferguson, yet again)

'The ref was diabolical. It was like he had a brand new
yellow card and he wanted to see if it worked.' (Richard
Rufus)

'Our passing was poor, we didn't get behind the ball, but I
still blame the referee.' (Bryan Robson, as Middlesbrough
crash 4–0 at Nottingham Forest)

'I know I've been banned for talking about officials, but these
days referees have no bottle, and I thought the linesman
was pathetic.' (Joe Kinnear)

'There are some people who have been making it difficult for
us to win in recent weeks, and they've been wearing black.'
(Trevor Francis, Birmingham City)

'The game was influenced by the referee and not by the
players.' (Ruud Gullit, Newcastle United)

'I got the yellow card this season for winking.' (Alan Shearer)

'I was once booked by a referee for shouting for the ball.'
(Johnny Giles)

'We had two players sent off at Newcastle last year for heavy
breathing.' (Joe Royle)

'I've seen harder tackles in the half-time pie queue than
the ones punished in games.' (George Fulston, Falkirk
chairman, on his side's poor disciplinary record)

'I'd like to get ten goals this season but the authorities don't
normally let me play for a whole season.' (Vinnie Jones)

'We prefer to lose because of the ability of the opposition
rather than the inability of the referee.' (Kenny Dalglish,
Blackburn Rovers)

'Three of their goals were offside.' (Malcolm MacDonald,

after Huddersfield Town go down 10–1 at Manchester
City)

'Four very strange decisions by the referee totally changed
the whole course of the game.' (Graeme
Souness, Liverpool, as they are hammered 5–0)

'I think the ref handed it to them.' (Alex Ferguson, after
Liverpool come back from a 2–0 deficit to draw with
Manchester United and threaten their stab at the
league title)

'The referee was absolute bobbins. And if you want a translation of bobbins, it's crap.' (Dave Jones, Southampton)

'Mr Reed was influenced by the status of the players ... the
referee asked how Posh Spice was, what they were eating
tonight and then sent our fella off.' (Jim Smith of Derby
County, implicating the streaky one in Stefan Schnoor's
sending off against Manchester United)

Taking responsibility involves adopting an internal perspective.
This is typified by Craig Brown, who, in the following quote,
starts an excuse but corrects himself: 'In every match we had a
penalty turned down which the replays confirm we should have
had. But I don't want it to sound like sour grapes. The bottom line
is that we weren't good enough.' Acknowledging the self as an
agency of change is important. Awareness and analysis of the part
played by the individual give rise to the prospect of change.
George Best, reflecting on his troubled career, stated that 'most of
the things I've done are my own fault, so I can't feel guilty about
them'. Perhaps with a hint of psychopathy, George unfortunately
arrived at the conclusion too late to save his career. The dawning
of awareness surfaced during the career of another genius with the
ball at his feet. Willie Johnston reflected, 'During my time in the
game I have been dismissed prematurely about 15 times, a statistic
I would prefer to ignore, but it takes an awful lot of ignoring.'

Once someone is aware of personal responsibility, the problem
is game for analysis. After being jeered off the pitch by the home
crowd following a draw with Middlesbrough during the early
stages of the season, the Arsenal coach Arsène Wenger speculated
that, 'Maybe we gave them too much last year [when his team won

the Double]. When you are used to caviar it is difficult to go back
to sausages.' Some less sophisticated stabs at taking responsibility
include:

'I think we just ran out of legs.' (David Pleat)
'Yes, they played well, but we played awful, which is a
   great leveller.' (Steve McMahon, as Swindon go out of
   the FA Cup to Stevenage)
'It was the first four goals that cost us the game.' (Dave Jones,
   as Southampton go down 4–2 at Chelsea)
'United were more dangerous when we had the ball than
   when they had it.' (Ruud Gullit, Newcastle United)
'We did enough to win, but that was not good enough.'
   (Kevin Ratcliffe)

Chapter 12

A positive spin

*'As one door shuts, another door opens –
no two ways about it.'*
Glenn Hoddle

There are always problems, uncertainties, dilemmas and difficulties. No manager is ever really free of doubt. Poor performances are inevitable. Not all players in a squad will gel together. Form is fundamentally ephemeral, with a player unpredictably and suddenly going flat. We may dwell on the bad deal and wallow in our sorrow, or seek to analyse the situation and find a positive perspective or option. Van Morrison, the legendary Irish songwriter, delivered this message in these words: 'Everything is an illusion. Nothing is real. Good or bad you can change it any way you want. You can rearrange it. Enlightenment.'

Being aware of the early signs of trouble is a talent. A team is sliding into adversity when:

- goal difference becomes negative,
- the number of points won becomes less than the number of games played,
- the team rises meteorically up the fair play league with an accumulation of disciplinary points,
- the team plummets in the form guide,
- home games are consistently drawn, and
- they fail to score on their travels.

A manager is in trouble when he succumbs to exasperation and defeatism, as illustrated here:

'It's driving me into sobriety.' (Jim Ryan of Luton Town,
   after a home defeat by QPR)
'We couldn't beat an egg.' (John Rudge, as Port Vale hit a
   losing stretch)
'I knew it was all over when the seventh goal went in.'
   (Danny McGrain of Arbroath, as they lose 9–1 to Celtic)
'When their second goal went in, I knew our pig was dead.'
   (Danny Williams, Swindon Town)

There are alternative ways of looking at any event. The schizo-
phrenic has a multifaceted view of the world, one in which the
perspectives are meshed and out of control. The sane stance is
more one of control and selection. Looking for a positive angle
makes sense. It involves a shift in the way we might typically look
at events. Are players, for example, seen as lazy or laid back? Do
they lack pace or sit in the hole and read the game? Do they make
six-yard tap-ins look easy or demonstrate the art of anticipation,
being in the right place when it matters?

Events that typically evoke misery, but could be construed from
a more positive angle, include:

Poor performances and results

A familiar cliché hinges on looking to the future, learning from the
débâcle of a 5–0 slaughtering and having the opportunity to put
things right for the next match. This was epitomised by Neville
Southall when he remarked, 'We've learned a few things and on
the whole it's been a good day', following the defeat of Wales by
Leyton Orient who were, at the time, placed 89th in the Football
League.

Other positive spins on terrible performances include:

'At least we were consistent.' (Barry Fry, manager of
   Birmingham City, after seeing his team miss all four
   penalties in a shoot-out against Liverpool)
'It might sound silly, but other than their three goals, Bolton
   did not create any chances.' (Terry Fenwick)

'We murdered them, 0–0.' (Bill Shankly)

'I consider this defeat to be the mother of future victories.'
(Antonio Oliveira, manager of Portugal)

'You sometimes learn more from your defeats.' (Ray
Harford, QPR)

'It's not the end of the world – just the end of Europe.'
(Roy Evans, as Liverpool crash out of the UEFA Cup
to Brondby)

'At the end of the day, it's not the end of the world.' (Jim
McLean of Dundee United, after losing the UEFA Cup
Final, suggesting a variant on the world's end theme)

'We've got one point from 27, but it's not as bad as that.'
(Alan Ball. Um, really?)

'Despite our bad run, we're playing some really good
football. Maybe we'll have to start playing badly to win.'
(John McGinley, Bolton Wanderers)

'Our away form this season may not be exceptional, but
compared to our home form it doesn't look bad at all.'
(Gary Mabbutt)

'A lot of hard work went into this defeat.'
(Malcolm Allison)

'And now with news of Scotland's 0–0 victory over
Holland… ' (Scottish TV reporter)

Relegation

Relegation is regularly construed positively. It may be considered as an opportunity for rebuilding or clearing out the uncommitted, over-paid 'dead wood'. Fans may welcome a season of visiting new grounds and sampling the meat and potato pasties of the lower divisions. As the Teessiders have sampled yo-yoing between divisions more than most, they have also mastered the positive spin:

'Although we have gone down, I don't think the players
should dwell on the negative side of it … we are back in the
position we were three years ago, but look how far we have
come.' (Nigel Pearson, Middlesbrough)

'Of course I made mistakes, because we were relegated …
It just means I have another challenge now – a new
challenge. This time we had three challenges – and lost
every one.' (Bryan Robson)

Player problems

George Best: 'We had problems with the wee fella, but I
prefer to remember his genius.' (Sir Matt Busby)
Matthew Le Tissier: 'You're never sure you want him playing
for you, but you're sure you don't want him playing against
you.' (Dario Gradi)

Opponents

'Underdogs are underdogs because they are not very good.'
(Johnny Giles)
'Sometimes you look at a defender and think, yeah, he's a big
lad. But when I see a big defender I think, great, he can't
turn.' (Michael Owen)
'Their team might have cost more, but ours is probably
worth more.' (Dario Gradi, comparing his Crewe
Alexandra side with Birmingham City)

Explaining your actions

'People have got me all wrong really. Underneath, I'm just
a big softie really.' (Neil 'Razor' Ruddock)
'I made a two-fingered gesture towards the fans to show
I had scored twice. It must have been misinterpreted.'
(Paul Peschisolido)
'You'd have to be on drugs to spit at Vinnie. He ran into it.'
(Darren Anderton, nervously parrying Vinnie Jones's
gobbing claim)
'Over the years there's been the odd hangover when I've had
to ring in with the old "it must have been something
I ate" excuse.' (Andy Townsend)

Errors

'A mistake is only a mistake when it is done twice.' (Arthur Cox, Derby County, taking a philosophical stance)

'Try missing one in the World Cup semi-final.' (Chris Waddle, seeking to help his Falkirk colleague Paul McGrillen take a different perspective after a penalty miss against Airdrie)

Bad decisions

'Yes, we could have had a spot kick, but I don't want to say too much because, after all, the referee did give us a couple of throw-ins during the ninety minutes.' (Tony Parkes, Blackburn Rovers)

'Bob Wilson often used to moan about Big Jack [standing on the goal line for corners] whose stock answer was, "Aye, I push him alright – usually with both his hands in my back."' (Pat Partridge, referee)

Seeing Yellow

'I was quite relieved [on getting booked] because everyone had been likening me to Lineker and saying I'd never get booked. I thought, good, that means I can start tackling now.' (Darren Anderton. When will he put his new found knowledge into practice?)

Team selection, being out of favour and being sacked

'I don't drop players – I make changes.' (Bill Shankly, Liverpool)

'We have no reserves at this club, only good players.' (Arsène Wenger, Arsenal manager)

'I've hardly played any football in the last three years, so I still feel fresh.' (Neil Webb, lacking first team football)

'The appeal of the job is that you are out on the edge and sometimes you fall off it, but at least you've been there.' (Howard Wilkinson)

Loss of players

'We'll be a better team without him, with more players
wanting goals.' (Bryan Flynn of Wrexham, after selling top
scorer Gary Bennett)

Injury

'Sometimes I think the injury was good. That I became a
better player out of it.' (Marc Overmars)

Personal abuse

'I take it as a compliment when people call me Quasimodo.'
(Peter Beardsley)

'They booed me because they loved me. I love that. If they
didn't boo me and they say nothing then they are really
saying "this player is invisible".' (David Ginola)

'The reason fans abuse me is because they are jealous'.
(David Beckham tries an old one, and in doing so
demonstrates the ability to probe the minds of millions.)
Accuracy is not the issue; rather, retaining self-esteem
through a sideways glance, a positive perception of
events, is.

Chapter 13

Mental strength

'Germany does not have better players, but even when they are under pressure, they seem to maintain a winning mentality.'
Franz Beckenbauer

The dawn of the realisation of the importance of mental toughness is over. Today there is a compelling momentum, a clamouring urge, to stress the attributes of resilience or mental hardness. As pressure for success and survival escalates, the need for 'crumple-free' players and managers operating in the flap-free zone heightens. This is well illustrated by George Graham, who admitted, when he took charge at Leeds United, that, 'It's important I get to know their character because I feel that mental attitude is second only to technical ability.' Graham proclaimed a similar view of the lofty eminence of mental toughness in the modern footballer as he took the helm at Tottenham Hotspur, announcing, 'I want a very strong mental attitude and, if I've got good technical players with that, then I'm on the right track.'

Mental strength is an elusive characteristic, hard to define yet readily accepted as important for the top player. Essentially, the gist of it is how effectively a player deals with pressure; how the array of eventualities that could potentially knock him off his game is handled. Is the player, faced with stressful incidents, racked with worry, a dithering mass of protoplasm, or does he face them with an inner strength, a determination to conquer in the face of adversity? Edgar Davids suggests he is cast as the latter: 'The higher the stakes, the tougher the fight, the better overall feeling I get. I can produce. I am a winner.'

There is a vast array of potential events that might affect a player. Importantly, it is worth considering that pressure is ultimately self-inflicted. Events, in themselves, are not the source of pressure. How successfully the event is handled determines the degree of pressure felt by player or manager. Pressure is truly a matter of perception. Steve Coppell was aware of this when he accounted for his premature resignation from Manchester City after 33 days in these words: 'I've suffered from huge pressure I've forced upon myself.' Kevin Keegan also made a similar point in saying, 'Pressure is what you put on yourself. When you set targets there's a pressure to reach them.'

Gordon Taylor typically offers an enlightened view of what is required, saying, 'We need now, in the modern game, to pay far more attention to psychology and making sure players' heads are right for dealing with the incredible pressure they're under.' The mind is, after all, designed for thinking, not worrying. Good players develop, sometimes intuitively, the ability to cruise unaffected through pressure situations. Great players turn it to their advantage.

A failure to consider and address the issue leaves players vulnerable and unable to perform to their potential. At the European Championships, Russian head coach, Oleg Romantsev, admitted, 'I have all the best players here tactically and technically, but I make the mistake of not considering their morale, spirit and mental preparedness.' However, Roy Evans, the Liverpool manager, revealed that there may be a limit to how much can be achieved through coaching and intervention: 'Our goalkeeping coach, Joe Corrigan, has done a fantastic job on David James's mental side. Though you'll never get that part completely right, because all keepers are mental anyway.'

We might conceptualise mental strength as the resourcefulness to avoid being distracted by a potentially stressful event. It involves a commitment to stay with the game. Ron Atkinson described Norman Whiteside as 'having the perfect temperament, remaining unfazed by the most demanding occasions'. Lawrie McMenemy said, 'Bruce Grobbelaar's so strong under pressure, I call him Crocodile Dundee.'

Players with mental strength tend to show something of the following:

- They visualise the potentially difficult situation by practising their future performance in the mind's eye. They picture what is required, then they go out and do it.
- They practise or simulate the potentially difficult situation. Practising penalties prior to a game that might conclude with a penalty shoot-out seems eminently sensible, but is amazingly often neglected. Playing friendlies before a major competition to acclimatise for humidity and heat is more usually considered in the modern game.
- They remain calm and collected, although perhaps not aware of the secret intimated by Gordon Strachan: 'You have to get used to the pressure. There's no release unless you're a Buddhist and can do meditation. They tell me that works.'
- They maintain a confidence in themselves that the situation poses no problem. 'What I have got from playing in England is a wealthy mental preparation that makes us get onto the pitch in the best frame of mind ... playing in England has given me total freedom of mind to express my best football,' said Gianfranco Zola.
- They are resilient, persistent, have bottle and tough it out. They come back against the odds. 'I was brought up to keep battling. You know, fight to the death and all that. It's a Yorkshire trait,' said gritty Neil Redfearn. Moving further north, Ian Durrant of Rangers claimed that, 'You need the balls of a rhinoceros to play in an Old Firm game.' Doubtless he was referring to courage rather than size.
- They reinterpret the eventuality in positive terms. Franz Beckenbauer noted that, 'A German can concentrate and pressure on him provokes performance, not paralysis.' The up and coming Dutch striker, Ruud van Nistelroy suggested, 'Pressure is something you need to keep your mind sharp and to keep you focused.' Marcel Desailly, in the face of prodigious French expectations to win the World Cup, claimed, 'The pressure gives us power.' He later

expanded on this theme by saying, 'I don't really get nervous for these games any more. I concentrate hard but I like the pressure that big games bring. The pressure has a positive effect. It brings the best out of me now where maybe before it would cause me to make mistakes.' Arsène Wenger, another French observer on the subject, remarked, 'I prefer the pressure at the top', while Ruud Gullit reframed crowd barracking in an exquisite fashion: 'If someone is booing me, I take it as a compliment because they are afraid of me. It makes me play better.'

- They are inspired by the pressure. Newspaper venom that slags off a player or his team will galvanise an effort to prove the critics wrong. They rise to the bait and invariably smear egg on the faces of those who criticise.
- They take control and stamp their authority on the game. They don't let the situation take control of them. 'Steve McMahon wants his team to control the game. Once he has the ball he's a dream. Teams get 70–80% of possession when he's in midfield,' said an admiring Alan Hudson.
- They dictate the play. 'There are road sweepers and violinists who make up a football team. Bruce [Grobbelaar] is a lead violinist,' mused Lawrie McMenemy in musical mood.
- They make the situation work for them. On their European travels, Liverpool invariably sought to silence the home supporters in the first 20 minutes by slowing the game and keeping possession. Their intention, of turning the home fans' hostility against their own team, worked over and over again.

Mental strength, as Rudyard Kipling might have proposed, is keeping your cool, when those around lose theirs. Dave Hill expanded this theme, describing the politics of the field of play:

- 'Rule One: don't retaliate when opponents bait you. The ref will send you off.
- Rule Two: don't lose your rag with the crowd when they shower you in spit ... when they goad you with monkey chants and throw bananas on the pitch.

- Rule Three: don't get upset when your own team-mates behave in exactly the same way.
- Break any of these rules, and they say you've got a temperament problem.'

Difficulties reveal the man. When players perform as if it means nothing when it means everything, they have the right temperament and character, and the admiration of every true football supporter. When David Batty missed a penalty against Argentina in the shoot-out that knocked England out of the 1998 World Cup, he lost no credibility because he showed bottle. He stepped up in that seething cauldron of hope, at best a novice of the spot kick, and took it with positive intent and expectation. On the other hand, David Beckham took the rap because, in contrast, he reacted to intimidation. He perfectly exemplified Dave Hill's rule one: he retaliated and was sent off.

Tell-tale signs of a fragile temperament or wavering of mental toughness occur when a player's head goes down, or when there is a faltering appearance of resignation in body language, a wide-eyed sense of trepidation of the big occasion, or reluctance and hesitancy in making a decision. 'My line isn't on the job,' said Ron Greenwood, the jumble of words indicating a distinct state of mental agitation. Dave Webb gave an interesting insight into Stan Bowles's mental state before a game, when he commented that 'Mentally he might be unprepared because he'd lost his money or had a row with his wife, but I never saw him worse for wear.'

Of the almost limitless number of potential hazards and pressures a player or manager may face, the following are just a few of those that are typically encountered. It is illuminating to note the contrast between those who succumb and those who rise above the pressure.

Living up to expectations

Of a father who excelled in the game:

- Jordi has struggled in vain to match Johan Cruyff's skill and eminence.

- Frank Lampard Jnr. made the grade, as did his father, with West Ham United.
- Jamie Redknapp did likewise, mirroring his father Harry's success.
- Darren Ferguson might give dad, Sir Alex, a run for his money.
- Paul will have his work cut out to live up to the standards set by Kenny Dalglish, although he did note that his dad 'wasn't a bad player really you know, average'.
- Andy Todd struggled to emerge from being Colin Todd's son, particularly when managed by him at Bolton Wanderers.
- Kevin had a real stab at matching father John Bond. 'Norwich's goal was scored by Kevin Bond, who is the son of his father,' we were enlightened by Frank Bough.
- Gavin, who is '5' 10", size ten feet, as elegant as footballers get; totally different to me, in other words', observed his father Gordon Strachan.

Of a coach:

'He's got the look of Denis Law about him, although I don't want to give Lee [Bowyer] a specific tag.' (Howard Wilkinson)

Changing room banter

'Enduring the mickey taking, as well as the media, hardly come into your head as things you will have to deal with when you dream about being a professional footballer.' (Tony Adams)

'Glenn Hoddle has a very, very tough persona, despite the fact that they used to call him Glenda.' (Peter Shreeves)

Intimidation on the field

'I'm lucky to have the temperament which means I don't react. I'm not unsettled by tough talk and I think that once your opponent resorts to that, then you know you've got him worried.' (Peter Beardsley)

'[Peter] Beardsley looked a great player, an absolutely brilliant player. I caught him with a couple of good early tackles early on – they were good tackles too – and he just got up, forgot about them and got on with the job.' (Peter Reid)

'The real hard men are people like Steve Bruce and Mark Hughes. They get battered and bruised every game but they just get on with it.' (Paul Ince)

'George Best was set upon by two defenders whose orders must have been to maim him. He took them on like a matador, weaving away out of distance of their savage tackles.' (Terry Neill, seeing George destroy the Uruguayans)

'Kenny Dalglish's kicked all the game long but I have never once seen him accept it and admit he was beaten.' (Graeme Souness)

'You couldn't frighten George Best. Plenty tried. He used to be kicked all over the park. When he was younger, he would just get up – if he could – shrug his shoulders, and get on with tormenting the opposition.' (Jim Baxter)

'George Best was like a wild stallion that everyone admired but no one could tame. You just couldn't get a rope round his neck. He was kicked … but it never interfered with his dedication to win and come back looking for more.' (Alan Ball)

'I could wade into Charlie George like a juggernaut and he wouldn't complain about it.' (Ron 'Chopper' Harris)

'You can't talk Denis [Law] off his game or get away with any of the usual pro tricks.' (Ron 'Chopper' Harris)

'Pelé was scared of nobody. He used to give it and take it. He was a genius.' (Tommy Smith)

'Jimmy Greaves took the ball player's lion's share of the rough stuff without complaint, though he had the knack of placing himself away from it and had the facility for making the offender look like a big clumsy oaf.' (Sir Matt Busby)

'I'm a more restrained player these days, in that I am not quite so prone to retaliation at provocation as I was.' (Billy Bremner)

'It's pointless bringing one's ability down to gutter level and thus handing the initiative to the opposition.' (Billy Bremner)

'I can cope with the physical problems. I have faced tough teams and defenders who kick you, but I've not let them intimidate me … skill is always more powerful than strength and it will always triumph.' (Juninho)

'They didn't hurt me. I am small but I am tough.' (Juninho)

'Tommy Smith came hammering across and knocked John Sissons clean over the low wall at Upton Park into the crowd … He picked himself up and came back to run Lawler and Smithy ragged. It was one of the sweetest sights I've ever seen.' (Bobby Moore)

'Steve Perryman and his mates didn't appreciate my style at all. Soon they were threatening to break me in half … probably thinking they would put this young whipper-snapper in order … I just ignored them. In turn they got more angry with me by the minute. That was the first lesson I learned at the top. Keep your mouth shut because the people doing all the talking are really the losers.' (Mark Hughes)

'Jimmy Case was very definitely a tough customer – the hardest of the lot in my opinion. Aggression, strength and a natural expertise for saving his own skin are all part of Jimmy's make up.' (Mark Hughes)

Difficult playing conditions

Dennis Bergkamp: 'When the fog, ice and cold arrive, he won't want to know.' (Alan Sugar, demonstrating a distinct lack of knowledge of Dutch weather)

'I just had to tell my boys to kick it. What's that got to do with football?' (Harry Redknapp, conjuring up a devious plan for playing Wrexham on an icy pitch)

Decisions going against you

'I just wonder what would have happened if the shirt had been on the other foot.' (Mike Walker, Norwich manager, puzzling over decisions going in Manchester United's favour)

'Only one person in the ground thought it was a penalty and he was the wrong one.' (Joe Royle)

Being the underdog

'Playing Liverpool: it was a case of barbed wire, building a dam and hoping for the best. They come towards you like a tidal wave.' (Steve Thompson, Charlton Athletic defender)

'Underdogs? I must tell you I do not like for me or my players to be called dogs.' (Bora Milutinovic, USA coach)

'In cup competitions, Jack will always have a chance of beating Goliath.' (Terry Butcher)

'We think we are a pub team. That's the way our mentality is – we will go anywhere and give anybody a game.' (Neville Southall, Everton)

Falling behind

'Going behind that early made it like trying to run uphill in treacle.' (Howard Wilkinson, Leeds United)

'We were too frail mentally. The goal killed the team and we seemed to have no legs after that.' (Gerard Houllier of Liverpool, after a home defeat by Leeds United)

'Five out of 10 for football. 11 out of 10 for character.' (Arthur Cox, when his team fought back to win after going 2–0 down)

'Hearts 2, Motherwell 0. A good fight-back there by Motherwell who were 2–0 down at one stage.' (Paddy Feeny)

Running out of games

'After Monday night there are only nine games left. That's
when the big clock starts ticking. And you can't beat the
clock.' (Alex Ferguson, surprisingly illustrating his point
with a timepiece metaphor)

A debut

'Within minutes my vision of life at the top was tarnished.'
(Lee Chapman)

'In my first Scottish Junior Cup tie, I'm playing outside left …
I look casually over to the right back … He looked like a
blend of King Kong, Ernest Borgnine and Bobby Shearer.
You have to say to yourself, "Ah, but a real player can
always make a monkey even out of a gorilla." That's good
in theory. It presupposes that you get tackled only when
you've got the ball.' (Jim Baxter)

'I'd just broken into the first team at Tranmere and had
scored two first half goals … Halfway through the second
half, Rochdale's centre-half sidled up to me and told me in
no uncertain terms that my goal scoring exploits had
finished for the day … A few minutes later a kick to the
genitals laid me out flat.' (Dixie Dean)

The big game

'I still think Cantona will let you down at the highest level …
in the big games he will go missing. He's a cry baby when
the going gets tough.' (George Graham)

'Eric [Cantona] is quite good in big games.' (Roy Keane,
taking an alternative viewpoint)

'Bobby Moore is made for the big occasion. The more
extreme the challenge, the more commanding he will be.'
(Ron Greenwood)

'Of course there have been emotional pressures. Why else
would he [Ronaldo] wake at four in the morning? He has
contracts to fulfil and suffers enormous pressures and

demands.' (Roberto Carlos, explaining Ronaldo's uncharacteristically lax performance in the World Cup Final and hinting at murkier goings on behind the scene)

Going into extra time

'I don't know how old I was at the start of that game, but I'm 93 now. We played for 120 minutes, but it felt like 120 years in Alcatraz.' (Martin O'Neill, Leicester, after a Coca-Cola Cup semi-final)

Penalties and shoot-outs

'I asked the players who wanted to take a penalty, and there was an awful smell coming from a few of them.' (Mick McCarthy, Millwall manager, after a shoot-out)

Away grounds and supporters

Intimidating, hostile, phlegm, cursing, mayhem: and that's just the scene in most tunnels before the players emerge. Crowds have been variously described as follows:

'A shrieking, whistling, fire-cracking mass of bias.' (David Lacey, describing a fairly typical Italian venue)
'I was frightened to death by the fans.' (Brian Laudrup, describing the Italian experience)
'Anfield equals apprehension for Chelsea.' (Martin Tyler)
'With the Everton fans there always seems to be a threatening attitude, a vicious undertone to their remarks. You never feel this is a football atmosphere – it creates more a sense of fear.' (Jack Charlton)
'Do they hate us? You go to take a corner at Elland Road and you've got 15,000 horrible skinheads in their end yelling murder at you.' (Ryan Giggs, endearing himself to the gentlemen of Leeds)
'If Cantona had jumped into our crowd he'd never have come out alive.' (Alex Rae, describing the New Den at Millwall)

'There are grounds where you know you'll be covered in spittle and you wear your old clothes.' (Dave Bassett)

The possible effect:

'We have a lot of young lads and playing at grounds like St James's is a problem for them.' (Steve Stone, Nottingham Forest)

'It used to be difficult to get a throw in at Anfield.' (Francis Lee)

'All over the world it would have been a penalty. But at Ibrox it wasn't.' (Ivan Golac, Dundee United manager, seeing his side denied a blatant spot kick)

The options:

Anfield: 'Playing here lifts good pros, but puts the bad 'uns under pressure.' (Bob Paisley)

'Sometimes it can be a bit intimidating, especially if you're a young lad coming into the team. I suppose you either love it or bottle it. And I love it.' (Ryan Giggs)

And how to rise above it:

'I must have done all right for them to gob all over me.' (Steve Jones, Bournemouth)

'Any player not inspired by that atmosphere should go and play golf with his grandmother.' (Clemens Westerhof, Nigeria coach in World Cup '94)

'If people have a pop you just have to get on with your game and try to prove them wrong.' (Julian Dicks)

'He's used to crowds – he's the youngest of thirteen kids.' (Howard Wilkinson, on Leeds United full back, Gary Kelly)

'I loved going to Anfield even though all you ever got was a cup of tea and a good hiding. You came away a bit wiser.' (Tommy Docherty)

'You heard that booing at the end? Well, I started it.'
(Ron Atkinson)

Home support and their demanding expectations

'The fans can lift us and inspire us to victory.' (Craig Brown,
Scotland)

'The advantage of being at home is very much with the home
side.' (Denis Law)

'The noise of a home crowd can be intimidating if you let it.
But you can use it as a source of energy.' (David Burrows,
Coventry City)

'Fans pay good money to watch you play and if you don't
perform well they've got a right to slag you off.' (Julian
Dicks)

'Alan Brazil allowed the crowd reaction to upset him so
deeply that, eventually, as a sub it looked like he preferred
to warm up in the tunnel. There was no rhino hide to
protect him from the barbs.' (Ron Atkinson)

'The problem with fans is that they apply pressure, which
forces you to bring in some other idiot who is going to
ruin the team.' (Alan Sugar)

Coping with success

'The pressure is greater when you're at the top because
people expect more of you.' (Jim Smith, Colchester United)

'We came back for the first day of training [after the
Championship win of 1973/74] and Shanks had us all in
together. "Thanks for last year, boys. Your medals are in
a box over there. Now forget it, we start at the bottom
again." He wanted men with the mental strength to do
that and it's difficult to keep doing that every single year.'
(Ray Clemence, Liverpool)

'Maybe you're not quite as hungry if you've won things.
You still want to win, you hate to lose, but it's not the first
time anymore and perhaps subconsciously you aren't so
desperate for it.' (Roger Hunt)

'When you inherit success, so much more is expected of you.'
(Jack Charlton, on why he wasn't attracted to clubs
topping their divisions)

Dealing with howlers

'You've got to be honest with yourself and hold your hands
up when you've made a mistake, but you can't let errors
prey on your mind. That's fatal.' (Tim Flowers, Blackburn
Rovers)

Coping with defeat

'Pressure is ten times greater when you are bottom of the
table.' (Benny Fenton, Millwall)

'Sometimes players forget what losing is like. They only
remember being winners. The alternative experience can
help the team develop.' (Alex Ferguson)

'Even when you're dead, you must never allow yourself just
to lie down and be buried.' (Gordon Lee)

'You get a lot of slaps in the face in this game and I think it
is fair to say this is another of them.' (Jim Leighton, after
Scotland lost 3–0 to Morocco)

Slumps in form

'We are on the crest of a slump.' (Jack Charlton,
Middlesbrough)

'The form is crawling its way back.' (Roy Evans)

'In terms of talent and ability Charlie [Cooke] was the best
we had … but Charlie had a mental problem. He had to feel
right on the day.' (Alan Hudson)

'What I always liked about Gary Lineker was the strength
and clarity of his mind. If he failed to score, he wouldn't let
it get him down. He'd make up his mind to go in there again
looking for chances.' (Terry Venables)

Savo Milosevic: 'I still believe he's a very good player, but
he must package all his attributes more regularly.' (Brian
Little, Aston Villa)

'As a striker, you are either in a purple patch or struggling.
At the moment, I'm somewhere in between.' (Bob Taylor)

'Form is just like a bird that passes by. Sometimes you have
it all the time around you. Sometimes it just flies away
and you don't know what the reason is.' (Ruud Gullit)

'Players say they found the tight collars around last season's
shirts restrictive, causing them to become frustrated,
leading to a lack of form.' (Julian Weatherall, Swindon
Town's marketing manager)

Being dropped

Joe Mercer once dropped a player – Mike Pejic – from the England
squad for being miserable: 'I've never seen him effing smile,' he
explained.

'It would take a mad axe-man running amok in the dressing
room for me to get back in the team.' (Colin Calderwood,
in somewhat defeatist mood at Tottenham Hotspur)

'The manager dropped Dennis Wise and the reason was valid
– he was playing crap. Nobody's guaranteed a place, there's
no favouritism.' (Ken Bates)

'He chose to retire. I was retired.' (Steve Clarke, reflecting
on Ruud Gullit's last game for Holland and his own final
outing with Scotland)

Typical reactions:

'With the arrival of Vialli, I could see that it might possibly
be a bit of a struggle to hold down a place in the side.'
(Paul Furlong, Chelsea)

'I always give the lads encouragement, but you have mixed
emotions. You want them to win, but how are you going
to get back in if they keep doing well?' (Jason Dozzell,
wistfully musing from the sidelines)

'I'm not surprised by his request. Some people who are out
of the team will try to fight their way back in; others will ask
for a transfer.' (George Graham, on Carlton Palmer)

The mentally strong:

'You have to be mentally strong to survive being dropped by your country and he [Zola] has reacted in a very positive way.' (Gianluca Vialli)

'Sometimes you have to get them mad to get a response. It was as if he was saying, "I'll show that little ginger sod that he was wrong to leave me out."' (Alan Ball)

'You've got to take the rough with the smooth. It's like love and hate, war and peace, all that bollocks.' (Ian Wright, on being restored to the England team)

'I'm a patient man, but I wouldn't like to be sitting on the bench for years.' (Tore Andre Flo of Chelsea, threatens)

Coping with the press and criticism

Criticism by the press can be construed as a professional foul – the writers go for the man, not the performance.

'It was never like this at Stafford Rangers. I was lucky to get one interview every six months there.' (Stan Collymore)

'The media vultures circle above Hoddle.' (Clive Tyldesly)

'Dealing with the media is an experience – if we had one reporter at Oldham it constituted a press conference.' (Joe Royle, on moving to Everton)

'I've reached a stage in life where I don't give a bugger what the press write about me, as long as it's not slanderous.' (Ron Atkinson)

'Why do people look at me and perceive me as a bad player or missing chances? You have to ask these people that.' (Andy Cole)

'I'm not fussed about the press because I couldn't give a monkey's what the press have got to say.' (Andy Cole)

'If people saw me walking on water, you can be sure someone would say, "Look at Berti Vogts, he can't even swim."' (Berti Vogts)

'You get turned over by the press now and again – it goes
  with the territory.' (David Platt)

'I don't think it takes a scientist to work out that if a team
  gets beat 5–0, it's a bit strange if the centre-forward takes
  the bulk of the criticism.' (Niall Quinn)

'My eldest son is playing in goal for Halifax reserves –
  and I think I've got pressure.' (Bobby Gould on being
  appointed manager of West Bromwich Albion)

Personal abuse

'Supporters need to maintain a psychological distance – a compassion gap. We can only maintain fanaticism [screaming at players] when the players are faceless functions of our own desires and fantasies,' said Rick Gekoski. When we know the players, or have even just asked for their autographs, we feel sorry for them and their mistakes and we refrain from verbal abuse.

'If someone in the crowd spits at you, you've just got to
  swallow it.' (Gary Lineker)

'Pressure is no excuse. I would take any amount of personal
  abuse for £10,000 a week.' (Sir Stanley Matthews,
  reflecting on Eric Cantona's reported salary)

'Jason [Lee]'s got to learn to take some stick. If he doesn't like
  it then there are two ways to cure it. Either he gets his hair
  cut or he scores more goals.' (Frank Clark)

'The English fans are wild with passion at every game and I
  love that, even when it means I get some abuse. Better that
  than to play in silence.' (Frank Leboeuf, Chelsea)

'Alex Ferguson's a master at psyching people out. But
  psychology won't work on us – we've got too many psychos
  in the side.' (Joe Kinnear)

On being a manager

'I wish Glenn Hoddle luck but he is putting his head in the frying pan.' (Ossie Ardiles, offering advice as Hoddle takes the England job)

Being a football manager is:

- 'like being in a mental asylum' (Bobby Gould, Wales)
- 'like a nitro-glycerine juggler' (Joe Royle, when asked what it felt like to manage Oldham Athletic)
- 'like strapping yourself into the electric chair for a while' (Neil Smillie at Wycombe Wanderers).

Or a player-manager:

'Player-management is violent exercise on top of a pile of worries.' (Alec Stock, Yeovil)

And what it can do to you:

'I'm not used to waking up in the morning and screwing the sweat out of my pyjamas.' (Graham Taylor, describing the pressures of managing England)

'I woke up this morning for the first time without a headache.' (Billy Bonds, after resigning from West Ham United)

'I'm almost afraid to look in the mirror in case my face is contorted. The fear of failure unsettles your life.' (David Pleat, Sheffield Wednesday)

'It's strange that Stan Collymore is being treated for stress. When I was his manager, it was me who had all the stress.' (Frank Clark, Nottingham Forest)

The high expectations:

'If Barca came second, that's failure.' (Louis Van Gaal, manager at Barcelona for a short time)

'The pressure is such that some coaches would love it if there were no matches.' (Claude Le Roy, Cameroon coach)

'The pressure is incredible. I can cope during the week but on match days I feel like my head is exploding.' (Kenny Dalglish, explaining his walk away from Liverpool)

Putting it into perspective:

'My electrician exam was tougher than this.' (Jimmy Case, Brighton)

'To me pressure is being homeless or unemployed, not trying to win a football match.' (Andy Roxburgh, Scotland)

Coping with injury

Injuries are unpredictable. Few players complete their career without some time out through injury. It does not necessarily happen on the pitch, as Michael Stensgaard, Liverpool's goalkeeper, proved. 'He was at home and he dropped the ironing board. He tried to catch it before it fell on the floor and he's dislocated his shoulder,' reported a dismayed Roy Evans. Other players seem prone to injury. Ian Marshall is one example, of whom Ipswich Town team-mate Mick McGiven said, 'His knee played up in the supermarket. He's not used to pushing the trolley.'

Denial is often the first reaction to injury. The player plays on. As Gary McAllister noted, 'I don't think a player ever plays 100 per cent fit now.' He plays with knocks and bruises, through pain and while needing a hernia operation. The player is frantically seeking to avoid losing his status, his place in the team, physical inactivity, social alienation and having to exchange changing room banter for the physio's room. He seeks to avoid the cognitive distress of not being fully in control but in the literal and metaphorical hands of the club doctor. Finally a player strives to avoid his fear of the future and the possible implications of injury: perhaps of not making it back, not regaining a place in the team or not being quite the dynamic player he once was.

Others – team-mates and coach – tend to ignore the injured player:

'He [Shankly] wouldn't speak to you. It was like putting a bell round your neck and walking round Melwood. His philosophy was that if he made injured players feel like lepers, they'd be back quicker.' (Ray Clemence)

'Kenny Dalglish uses psychology: when you're injured he
won't even speak to you, won't ask how you are. I think it
comes from Bill Shankly: "You're no use to me if you're
injured."' (Graeme Le Saux)

'Managers don't need to speak to injured players because
they're not part of their plans.' (Tom Cowan, Huddersfield
Town)

However, Bob Paisley used injury as an opportunity. He said, 'I
find out more about a player when he's injured. However much
you try to involve him, he seems an outcast. You see the reaction,
the character when a player is down.' Good recovery from injury
is dependent on good medical care and the involvement of physio-
therapy. It is equally important to have the mental capacity to put
the injury in perspective, to take control through monitoring
progress, to use the free time to work on areas such as other
muscle groups, tactics and diet, and to stick with a determination
to overcome the problem. Always dream of being back, as
Ronaldo intimated by saying, 'I feel like a fish not a soccer player. I
want to smell grass not chlorine', as he tired of rehabilitation in
the swimming pool.

'People ask me "How do you keep smiling?" I just know
if I didn't, I'd go doolally flip.' (Gary Phillips, Barnet
co-manager)

Chapter 14

Confidence

*If you're confident, you're always totally different
to the player that's lacking confidence.'*
Ossie Ardiles

The outward signs of confidence are reasonably easy to detect. Players like Dwight Yorke or Nigel Martyn smile, even when the game seems to pass them by, in contrast to the despair-furrowed brow that so habitually bedecks Andy Cole's face. Confident players carry themselves with composure, poise and relaxed ease, rather than the awkwardness of a giraffe with dyspraxia. They do the basics well, hitting volleys with ease, controlling the ball with a first touch, creating time or hypnotising a bemused defender with an audacious shimmy. Confident players want the ball, make themselves available and influence the pattern of the game by reading the play, directing others and taking control.

Self-assured players also tend to do the difficult well. They hit a 40-yard pass with the ease of a two-foot lay-off, nutmeg a close and intent marker with comfort or place a penalty inside the post in the style of a Johnny Giles. They will stand still and create space à la Gascoigne, lob an advancing goalkeeper as Suker did against the eclipsing presence of Peter Schmeichel, and control, juggle and dispatch a swerving cross in the mode of Dennis Bergkamp. 'Good players allied to supreme self-confidence make for an unbeatable combination,' said Brian Hall of Liverpool.

The really confident player take risks, perhaps doing the unorthodox, like an artist secure about the basics and keen to experiment with novel and original ideas. They are innovators, the vanguard of reform. Cruyff's dazzling feints, Blanco's surprising two-footed jump-dribble, Higuita's scorpion kick, Pelé's step over and Frank Worthington's swivel volley are all examples of the actions of players with a rich and consistent vein of self-belief.

Despite all the outward signs, confidence is a belief. It occurs when we judge ourselves to have the ability to complete a task successfully. We have the know-how to know how to perform. Fascinatingly, some players may appear self-assured but lack real inner belief. Kenny Dalglish was one such player. He admitted, 'One of my weaknesses as a footballer was a shortage of self-belief. If I had had more self-confidence I would have been a better player, and maybe a better manager as well.' In many ways, confidence is a contrast and anathema to anxiety or nervousness. Whatever eventuality faces a player, he does not anticipate the worst, but figures he has the capacity to assuredly deal with it in a positive way. Confidence is:

A deep sense of belief in one's ability

'I know only one way to take penalties: to score them.'
   (Eric Cantona)
'I believe I could play in Brazil's national team and not feel
   uncomfortable.' (Matthew Le Tissier)
'I think it is important to be aware of your skills, not have
   any doubts about anything, feel good about it and go for it.'
   (Ruud Gullit)
'I was supremely confident on the field. That was my stage.
   Give me the ball and I could do anything with it, yet I've
   never been that comfortable around people.' (Tony Currie)
'I think I'm in the side on merit. I wouldn't pick myself
   otherwise.' (Jimmy Quinn, Reading player-manager)
'When I see all my legs out, I have confidence. I look at my
   muscles and they look big and I feel strong. With big shorts,
   I can't see my muscles at all.' (Paolo Di Canio, explaining
   his affection for short shorts)
'I have complete faith in my ability because I know I'm a top
   quality player.' (Davor Suker)
'Our players didn't think they were the best – they knew it.'
   (Steve Staunton, Liverpool)

'God created me to delight people with my goals.' (Romario)

'Long after I pack the game up, I'll be able to tell my kids I was one of the best players in the Premiership. That might make me sound like a big-headed twerp, but it's true.' (Matthew Le Tissier)

'Nottingham is a beautiful city with lovely people. The Trent is lovely too. I know, I've walked on it for 18 years.' (Brian Clough)

If not the tops, then on at least an equal footing with others

'Don't think you are worse than the other players, don't look up to them. Think you are just as good as them because you are and if you think they are better, you are not going to make it.' (Aaron Winter to Jimmy Floyd Hasselbaink as he is included in the Dutch World Cup squad)

Self-realisation

'I don't want to be remembered as just another player. I want to go down in the history of world football.' (Ronaldo)

'I always knew I could play. I didn't need anyone to tell me. I was self-assured, even when I was a young kid. I did what I thought was right.' (Charlie George)

Not being dented by circumstances or ineptitude

'I have not lost confidence in myself one iota.' (Brian Clough, after a series of disastrous signings)

Not being fazed

'Kenny Burns didn't give a toss about anybody or anything. He wandered around the dressing room in exactly the same cocksure frame of mind, whether we were playing Liverpool or Lincoln.' (Brian Clough)

'Peter Osgood's greatest asset was his supreme confidence. He would take the field knowing he was going to score and

he didn't give a monkey's who he was playing against.'
(Alan Hudson)

Being positive

'At any level you'll always get a chance.' (Ron Atkinson)
'We can beat anyone on our day – so long as we score.'
  (Alex Totten, Kilmarnock)
'I knew that some of the Celtic support thought I was past
  my sell-by date and it is at times like those that negative
  thoughts consume people's minds. It's what a player
  cannot do that becomes the issue instead of what he might
  be good at.' (Charlie Nicholas at Celtic, making a valid
  point in the face of a wave of hostile reactions)
'You've got to believe that you're going to win and I
  believe that we'll win the World Cup until the final
  whistle blows and we're knocked out.' (Peter Shilton,
  perhaps not fully grasping the implications of what
  he is saying)

Not being afraid to make mistakes

'When you're feeling confident and the crowd is with you,
  you feel free to express yourself, not afraid to make
  mistakes.' (John Salako)
'Lee Dixon's biggest asset is that he is not afraid to fail.'
  (George Graham, Arsenal)

'Confidence is not something that players can get by taking a
tablet,' said Dave Bassett, somewhat dogmatically, when he ruled
at Nottingham Forest. Confidence is inescapably a psychological
notion and therefore requires a psychological framework to
understand how it develops.

The concept of confidence is steeped in construction metaphor.
We build confidence through the recognition of our endeavour in
achieving success. It is perhaps appropriate to consider positive
experiences as the breeze blocks and a recognition of ourselves as
causal being the mortar holding the edifice together. Confidence

arises from sifting past experiences for evidence of excellence and declaring ownership. One interesting method of building confidence is the creation of a video with a compilation of a player's 'great moments', for him to peruse at leisure.

More mundane approaches lean on encouraging players to focus on construing recent impressive or noteworthy experiences, particularly in areas of improvement, previous performances and preparation. 'Doing tricks gives you confidence,' said David Ginola with a simple formula. A Tottenham team-mate offers a different view, with Ramon Vega claiming, 'We began to keep clean sheets and that made the difference to the team's confidence' once George Graham arrived to impose his style. Building confidence, of course, relies on players having ability. As Bill Nicholson of Tottenham Hotspur said, 'If a player is not a good player, no amount of kidding or psychology will make him one.'

The manager's role has traditionally been considered pivotal in building confidence. The following players endorse this:

> 'The manager has given us unbelievable belief.' (Paul
> Merson at Aston Villa under John Gregory)
> 'Glenn Hoddle was the best manager I ever had. He just said,
> "You are the best in your position, now go out and play."
> He helped me mentally and he gave me a lot of confidence.'
> (Dan Petrescu at Chelsea)

Managers also appear to believe confidence building is a core attribute of their armoury:

> 'I've made my career by getting players nobody else wanted
> and getting them to believe that they are the bollocks.'
> (Barry Fry, Birmingham City)
> 'I took him [Le Tissier] out on to the golf course and I let him
> beat me. He took £17.50 off me and I am sure it helped
> boost his confidence.' (Dave Jones, Southampton manager)

Having a quiet unassuming belief in your ability often goes unrecognised. Players display it on the park in the way they play. They avoid arrogance by keeping their belief to themselves. When confronted they might avoid the issue or underplay their strength of belief with a tongue-in-cheek comment like the following:

'When I joined Rangers I immediately established myself as third-choice left-half. The guys ahead of me were an amputee and a Catholic.' (Craig Brown)

'I'm sure our name's on a cup somewhere, but it will have a saucer with it.' (Brian Laws, Scunthorpe United)

'People will think I'm crackers. I'm voluntarily going back into the madhouse.' (Trevor Francis, on joining Birmingham City)

In a strange show of logic, Brian Clough explained, 'I call myself "big 'ead" to remind myself not to be one.' Over-confidence leads to complacency on the pitch and arrogance in communication. The underdogs always have a chance because their better opponents can tend to underestimate the task and overestimate their ability. Confidence is only ever one element of the blend of success, and inferior players and teams in terms of ability and belief in ability can succeed with determination, concentration, teamwork and the like.

The hesitant, fearful, self-conscious and ill-composed reactions of those lacking self-belief are all too apparent. Poor ball control, missed chances, late tackles and mistimed passes happen with some regularity. Yet confidence begins to sap only when a player makes too much of such events. When we focus on errors, we undermine a belief in our ability, we increase mistakes and confidence is destroyed.

'It's the thing between the ears that matters – confidence.'
(Terry Venables)

Chapter 15

Emotional control

'If you want to play well you have to feel good in the head.'
David Ginola

Emotions are inevitable. They make up the fabric of everyday life. A football pitch, as a microcosm of life, is a maelstrom of feelings. The ecstasy of a screaming 25-yard volley that ricochets in off the bar, the euphoria of holding the cup aloft or the more covert pleasure in timing an accurate cross are all emotions of a positive kind. The humiliation of ballooning a gilt-edged chance over the bar, the frustration of a misdirected pass and the anger of a manager trying to influence a tactical change as his charges resemble an ill-coordinated batch of headless chickens are feelings of a more negative ilk.

Emotions appear to invade. They catch us unawares. Yet they are an expression of our psyche. They arise when events threaten the way we see ourselves. We feel frustration with a rank bad cross because it endangers a view that we are competent in this regard. We feel nervous entering the tunnel on our debut because we fear a bad performance will affect our future career with the club. We feel elated with a perfect last-ditch tackle because it validates or, perhaps, exceeds what we thought ourselves capable of.

However, positive or negative, expressed emotion is baggage. It saps strength and distracts a player's focus. Terry Venables illustrates the fatigue of emotions in reflecting on Paul Gascoigne's performance in the infamous Spurs v. Arsenal FA Cup semi-final: 'I thought he would have lasted ninety minutes, but he used up so much energy in the dressing room, he knocked himself out.' As for emotions distracting a player's concentration, it is now entrenched football folklore that a team is at its most vulnerable immediately after scoring.

Emotions are problematic when players fail to take control. On the field emotions should be fleeting. When players hold on to the feeling their game is disrupted. Players, of course, intuitively know this and sometimes seek to niggle an opponent to frustrate and anger them with the intent to spoil their focus. Ecstasy and the torment of errors should be treated similarly. Admit them and let them go. Arsène Wenger applauds Dennis Bergkamp for the way he controls his emotions on the field: 'He has a passionate side – he just doesn't show his emotions.'

The wide array of emotions probably all arise from one source – adrenaline. We colour the surge of adrenaline by the way we perceive the event. We anticipate failure and feel nervous; we are clattered by a late tackle and see the red mists of anger. Emotions have three facets – somatic, behavioural and cognitive.

Somatic emotion refers to bodily changes. The stomach churns, the heart beats hurriedly and sweat glands erupt like Jim Smith's top lip. Behavioural aspects include the slumped shoulders of dejection, the raised fists of a handbag confrontation and the furrowed brow of perplexity that frequently descends upon the striker's face as another chance is scuffed. Finally, cognitive aspects include worry, retribution and catastrophic thoughts of possible failure.

Nervousness is a frequent pre-match visitor. The bigger the game, the greater the sense of anxiety. Jorge Cadete of Celtic described the Old Firm game as being 'dominated by nerves'. George Best gave a vivid, if not over complimentary, picture of a colleague's physiological reaction to nerves: 'Alan Gowling was sick, violently sick. He would throw up in the toilet before a game.' In the manager's case, nerves may be a constant partner throughout the pre-match build-up and the match itself. Alan Hansen realised he wasn't cut out to be a manager because, as he said, 'At 2.15 on a Saturday I used to go back and forth to the toilet 45 times.' Mick McCarthy testified to the anxiety that goes with the dug-out: 'At 2–1 down, my heart was pounding and I was feeling as sick as the proverbial donkey.'

Nervousness is energy that a player construes as bad. He may anticipate the match with apprehension, sensing he'll fall short of the mark and fail to do himself justice; he may yearn to avoid the experience and dread that a fragile self-esteem will be shattered. Avoidance or the desire to avoid is often a behavioural response. Dennis Bergkamp, because of a specific fear of flying, literally had an escape clause written into his contract. As Arsène Wenger, his Arsenal manager, reflected in preparing the team for a European Championship trip to Panathinaikos without his star striker, 'The only way he will fly to Athens is if he turns into a pigeon.' Worry is the anticipation of disaster. It is the thinking man's expression of nervousness, perhaps that the player will be made to look stupid. 'A lot of fear surrounds playing for England. Players are frightened about being ridiculed for making errors,' said Tim Flowers of Blackburn Rovers and sporadically England.

Players may seek to counter nervousness resulting from any of the three facets – somatically, behaviourally or cognitively. Relaxation counteracts the somatic effects of nerves. Michael Thomas would drop off to sleep before a match. According to George Best, his team-mate Bobby Charlton found a more debatable means of counteracting pre-match nerves: 'He used to have a couple of shots of whiskey before he went out.' Trevor Sinclair finds another way of relaxing: 'There's a lot of shouting in the QPR dressing room before a match, but I just try to relax. I go into the toilets and read the whole programme.'

Remaining calm, composed, cool, collected and patient is a behavioural response to the potential restlessness of nerves. The following examples reflect these attributes on the pitch:

> 'Jimmy Greaves was always very calm, very collected and, where scoring goals was concerned, he was a Picasso.'
> (Clive Allen, budding art critic)
> 'Gareth Barry is so wonderfully cool and composed and splendidly ready to go forward in attack.' (Brian Glanville)
> 'Pat Jennings had the nerve of a bomb disposal officer.'
> (Eamonn Dunphy)
> 'Michael Owen really is remarkable in the way he retains his cool at all times.' (Steve Double)

'George Best had ice in his veins.' (Danny Blanchflower)
'Ronaldo has the brain of a refrigerator.' (Brian Moore)

Averting pre-match nerves often involves players developing routines. 'I would pick up a programme, take it to the toilet and read it. I would come out and walk out of the dressing room and go and talk to my friends outside … there was nothing to worry about,' remarked George Best, describing his pre-match routine. Sometimes routines evolve into superstitions. Quirky acts serendipitously become linked with a good result and a superstition is born. Players then dread giving up the routine for fear of catastrophic consequences. They lace their boots a particular way, touch the post at a corner or come out of the tunnel last, pulling on a shirt à la Paul Ince. There are many other interesting superstitions:

'I don't have any pre-match superstitions or habits, but I always have my packet of chocolate buttons.' (Peter Beardsley, both denying and admitting to a superstition in the same breath)

'I always feel quite lucky going into a game if Catherine has just shaved my head. Every time she did that at Oxford I seemed to score a goal.' (Matt Elliott)

'I always used to put my right boot on first and then obviously my right sock.' (Barry Venison. Obviously, that is, if you wish to dress like some deranged fashion guru)

'I always take my right boot off at half time as the circulation around the big toe isn't too good. I like to give it a little wiggle.' (Matt Elliott again, at Leicester City)

'I don't have lucky signs except my teeth. Sometimes I play with them in and sometimes out.' (Martin Chivers, indicating an affection for the offbeat)

'Nobby Stiles used to take out his teeth, put his contacts in, check his kit and then check it again. It would take him an hour to get ready.' (George Best, maintaining the dental theme)

'Bobby Lennox would have his lucky suit. By the end you could almost see your face in the arse of his trousers.' (Jimmy Johnstone, his team-mate at Celtic)

Craig Short of Everton gave up his routine and where did it get him? He said, 'I used to have all sorts of superstitious routines that I went through prior to kick off, but that was getting me nowhere, so I just sit and panic before a game now.'

Addressing nerves cognitively means substituting any negative thoughts with positive ones. This was illustrated (perhaps not that well) by David Batty prior to the penalty miss against Argentina in the World Cup. He said, 'There were no nerves at all. I just had positive thoughts.' An alternative is to re-frame the energy, by considering the adrenaline a positive, not a negative, force. Perhaps construing the energy as excitement, an indication of readiness or a preparedness to compete. 'Of course I wasn't nervous. Taking a penalty to win the Cup is what you are in the game for. If you don't feel excited by that, perhaps you should not be a professional footballer,' proclaimed Eric Cantona

Anger and annoyance are recurrent emotions on the field. Somatically and metaphorically there are raised temperatures, short fuses, simmering anger, hot-headed reactions, perhaps a rush of blood, seeing the red mist and flashes of temper. Here are a few examples:

'[Mark] Hughes quickly disappeared in the red mist of frustration and anger that so often envelops him.' (Russell Kempson)

'It's really a case of him losing les marbles.' (Gary Lineker, after Eric Cantona's infamous kung-fu kick at a supporter)

'When Eric [Cantona] feels an injustice, he has to prove to the whole world that he's been wronged. He can't control his temper. That's just part of his game.' (Alex Ferguson)

'I allowed myself to be provoked by the infamous Leeds tactics, first an off-the-ball whack from Johnny Giles followed soon afterwards by a crafty dig from Bremner that brought on the red mist of temper.' (Kevin Keegan, after being sent off)

'In the early days my temper was very quick. Now it takes a lot to get me riled.' (Francis Lee)

'Most people's fuses go off once in a while, but Neil [Ruddock]'s would go off several times in one game.' (Jimmy Case)

Roy Keane: 'He gets the red mist in front of his eyes and goes
    looking for them.' (Larry Lloyd)

Behaviourally, anger is noticeable in petulance, swearing,
tantrums, handbags at two paces, getting at each other's throats
and dishing it out with both barrels. A few confessions and obser-
vations from on and off the field:

'I completely lost it. I went mad, berserk. I lost my rag big
    time. I was shouting and swearing. I couldn't believe the
    injustice of it. I admit I kicked the door, kicked the furni-
    ture. I was crying and out of control.' (Paul Gascoigne,
    reacting to his exclusion from the 1998 World Cup squad)
'Alex [Ferguson] always had a hot temper. He'd have caused
    a fight in an empty house.' (Martin Ferguson, his younger
    brother)
'I can't speak English when I get really angry.'
    (Gianluca Vialli)
'Players like myself, Roy Keane and Eric Cantona can dish it
    out but it's just our natural aggression.' (Paul Ince)
'Of course it was wrong of me to do what I did [deck referee
    Paul Alcock] but I couldn't control myself any longer.'
    (Paolo Di Canio)
'I'm very placid most of the time, but I blow up very quickly.
    I shout and wave my arms, and my lip twitches. I become
    incoherent and I swear. All at the same time.' (Jack
    Charlton)
'I could never get on with Bremner. It was like a red rag to a
    bull.' (Clive Thomas, referee)
'The ref gave a goal against us and as I turned around I saw
    this big furry microphone so I laid into it. I kicked it and it
    went spinning around like a boomerang and landed 20
    yards away. Then the Sky touch-line reporter came up to
    me and said, "So, Mick, you must be disappointed."'
    (Mick McCarthy)
'Lee Ashcroft's a bit of a loony and he can be bad tempered.'
    (Alan Buckley, West Bromwich Albion)

Eruption of anger disrupts a player's performance. Particularly with the emergence of cameras extracting all the action from all the angles, players have to increasingly show restraint. Retaliation, a dig off the ball, in-your-face verbals and a mouthful of venom are all picked up, magnified and studied at great length by the pundits. Yet the crux is the effect on performance. Anger distracts the player's focus from what he should be doing. Taking control over the red mist is essential.

Pelé was a model of restraint. He intimated that a failure to control your temper leaves you with a liability. 'I lose my temper very often, but I try my best not to show it, especially not to an opponent during a game. It gives him an advantage,' he reflected. Another paragon of self-control, Arsène Wenger, described himself: 'I don't kick dressing room doors, or the cat – or even journalists.'

Paul Devlin has been less successful as regards restraint: 'I have to learn to keep my temper in check. Sometimes it boils over through frustration ... but I'm trying to cork it and I think I'm getting better.' Other attempts to curb the flames with dubious success include:

'Cantona's so mild mannered when the volcano is not
   erupting inside him.' (Alex Ferguson)
'I have learned to control myself, but occasionally things do
   go on and I react in the heat of the moment.' (Paul Ince)
'When I'm on the pitch I'm a different animal, and that's an
   animal I'm trying to keep controlled now.' (Ian Wright)

Dejection is a common sight on the field and frequently, after a poor performance, in the dressing room after a game. It is the stunned reaction to a blunder, defeat, dismissal or being dropped from the team. 'The despair when you lose in football goes very deep. There is no such deep emotion when you win,' noted Peter Eustace of Sheffield Wednesday. Gordon Strachan, in similar tone, observed, 'The feeling after a win is never as intense as after a bad loss. A defeat hurts more and lasts longer.' Kevin Keegan also remarked on the contrast: 'Winners can laugh but losers have to make their own arrangements.'

The deep mysterious feelings of despair are often reflected in metaphors of fallen crests, sick parrots and gutted beings. But there are other ways:

'Gary Ablett there… wringing his head with disappointment.' (Jimmy Greaves)

'Frank Stapleton – in the sad art of grumbling, he was world class.' (Ron Atkinson)

'I was disappointed they got a cross in. I was disappointed we were done at the back stick. I was disappointed Shearer stuck it in the net. Apart from that, I'm as happy as Larry.' (Peter Reid)

'If I get sulkers around the football club, I'll have them out of here so quickly it's untrue.' (David O'Leary, Leeds United)

'How do I feel? Lower than a snake's belly. That's how I feel.' (Steve McMahon, after Swindon Town are relegated)

'If you cut me open and had a look inside right now it wouldn't be a pretty sight. I don't know if I can sink any lower.' (Gary McAllister, after Seaman saved his penalty in the Euro '96 England v. Scotland clash)

'No matter how I look at it, or how much the other players console me, I'm still left with the feeling that I let everybody down.' (Gareth Southgate, after his penalty miss in Euro '96 that denied England a place in the final)

'In terms of the Richter Scale, this defeat was a force eight gale.' (John Lyall, West Ham manager)

'I'd hang myself but we can't afford the rope.' (Iain Munro, Hamilton Academicals manager)

'Everyone is feeling a little low, but no one is feeling down.' (Howard Kendall, in a somewhat mysterious tone)

'The hardest thing is when we lose. A year ago I'd have gone out and had a drink, but now I have to talk to people.' (Paul Merson, on the wagon)

'I'm dreadful when we lose. Really bad. I didn't go out for about six weeks.' (Steve Lomas)

'I felt so ashamed after being booked, realising that I've lost my self-control again and failed once more in simple human understanding.' (Ossie Ardiles)

Ecstasy, in contrast, is the emotion of accomplishment, the buzz of achievement. This is typified by Stuart Pearce, energised into a shudder of euphoria after scoring a penalty for England in Euro '96 to purge the memories of a semi-final miss in similar circumstances six years earlier. Pelé perceived a correlation where 'The more difficult a victory, the greater the happiness in winning.' This was effectively reiterated when the Romanian coach, Anghel Iordanescu, reflected on how victory in the World Cup would be viewed in the homeland: 'Beating Argentina is the greatest moment for our people since the revolution.' Alan Buckley chose an interesting set of metaphors to describe his team's reaction to victory: 'The boys' feet have been up in the clouds since the win.' Joe Royle picked perhaps an even quirkier one when he remarked, 'I'm like a dog with two dicks' after Everton took the points at Chelsea. Jimmy Nicholl claimed, 'This would bring a tear to a glass eye' after Raith Rovers beat Celtic to lift the Scottish League Cup.

The sense of exhilaration experienced when a player walks out in front of a cheering crowd thousands strong, or receives a standing ovation on leaving the field following a blinder is encapsulated by George Best. He said of emerging from the tunnel at Old Trafford, 'I can still recall the hairs on the back of my neck stood up. I was numbed. At the same time I felt exhilarated. There was no fear, however, not for a moment. And there never would be.'

The feeling of scoring a winning goal, side-stepping three defenders or nutmegging a bruising full back in front of a bank of loyal and devoted fans is almost inescapably described in orgasmic terms:

> 'If we win, it'll be a nation-wide orgasm.' (Jesus Gil of Athletico Madrid, eagerly awaiting the game with Real Madrid)
> 'If it was a straight choice between having sex and scoring a goal, I'd go for the goal every time. I've got all my life to have sex.' (Andy Gray)
> 'The surge of adrenaline was so strong, I could have done anything at that moment … It's like when you feel the blood pumping through your neck when you're having sex.

Scoring a goal like that was an incredible high, almost
surrealistic. Your head explodes.' (Rodney Marsh, on
firing in a gem to equalise for QPR at Wembley)

And with a twist, Gordon Strachan dispelled an apparent truism
by suggesting that it is possible to experience two different
emotions at the same time. On narrowly avoiding relegation with
Coventry City, he said in all seriousness, 'We were disappointed at
being so excited.'

Chapter 16

Communication

'And Bilic says to him, "I think you've
over-reacted a bit there, old chap."'
Brian Moore

Commentator Brian Moore's lip-reading of Croatia's Slaven Bilic's comment to a Turkish forward approximates a meta-communication – a communication about a communication. It reflects the essence of the interaction between the two players, but also illustrates much that is problematic about the art of commentary. It is an interpretation of the event, and a sanitised one at that. Is Bilic in all likelihood going to express himself to a Turk in the language of an old buffer? The language is Moore's own, and tells us as much about him as the altercation on the field of play. It is also probable that the important message conveyed by Bilic is not verbal – would he expect the offender to translate Croat into Turkish? – but non-verbal. Bilic's expression, body language and the venomous nature of his outpourings convey the intended message.

Non-verbal communications are universal and widespread on planet football. Referees employ a whistle to stop and start play. They use arm gestures to relay the type of free kick, the awarding of a goal or the need for a wall to be ten feet back at a free kick. The colour of a piece of card produced from the top pocket is understood universally to mean a booking or dismissal.

Similarly, managers communicate a great deal through their expression and gestures. Tony Adams said of his Arsenal manager George Graham, 'I would probably have eaten him alive as a centre-forward but the body language off the pitch, what with that Scottish mask of his, definitely said, "I'm the boss. Be careful."' Players bawl and shout, but also convey their wishes by gesture. Defenders organise the back line with arms outstretched, goalkeepers indicate the size and placing of a wall with fingers aloft, and clumsy full backs disdainfully seek to persuade the referee that a flattened winger dived by some rapid rotating arm movements.

Non-verbal communications are so automatic they relay a player's true feelings. Those who think they are offside on scoring a goal invariably glance at the linesman before erupting into celebration. Those who trip an advancing forward in the penalty area automatically and anxiously look to the referee before suggesting a dive.

It is an axiom that communication is two-way. Danny Wilson of Sheffield Wednesday hinted at the difficulties that may arise when languages are not shared, by suggesting in relation to Paolo Di Canio that, 'He understands me and I think I understand him.' Announcements without a receiver are just drivel.

> 'I didn't listen to anybody unless I believed in them. Malcolm Allison was probably the only coach I've ever played for who made any sense so I ignored all the others.' (Rodney Marsh)
> 'I listen to players, but that doesn't necessarily mean that I take any notice of them.' (Bryan Robson)
> 'Jason [Euell] has been able to pass on good advice. The most important thing he told me was not to always take notice of the manager.' (Carl Cort, Wimbledon)
> 'You can hear what they're saying. The art is pretending you can't. You've enough problems out there as it is.' (Alan Hudson, providing an insight into his relationships with managers)

As fans we scream instructions from the terraces, yet it can barely be thought to make a jot of difference. Rather than seeking to influence the play, are we communicating our thoughts and feelings to other supporters around us, looking for support for our ideas? As fans, our efforts make a difference when we communicate *en masse*. Our presence is noted, as demonstrated in Barry Davies's description of a mass of Dutch fans as 'looking rather like a huge jar of marmalade'. We chant and sing in unison to energise and lift the team; we protest towards the directors' box when dissatisfied by the current manager.

'If our Anfield fans at Wembley can make as much noise as at home, I don't think there's a team in the world that can live with Liverpool.' (Bill Shankly, before the 1965 FA Cup Final)

'St James's Park and Elland Road are very similar crowds. But I'd have to say Newcastle are the most fanatical – even the grannies sing.' (David Batty)

'At Newcastle the crowd is worth one and a half goals' start to the home side, but here at Southend it's probably minus six.' (Vic Jobson)

'We have the greatest fans in the world, but I've never seen a fan score a goal.' (Jock Stein)

'The last time a team in Scotland lived up to the fans' expectations was in 1960 when Real Madrid beat Eintract Frankfurt in Glasgow [in the European Cup Final].' (Andy Roxburgh)

On the pitch, some players seem to be intriguingly tuned into each other. They appear to be on the same wavelength, to anticipate just what team-mates are about to do, to read the pass and almost telepathically know the position of a striking partner. 'Great striking partnerships come in pairs,' said Nigel Spackman, stating the patently obvious. When partnerships fail it is often due to a lack or breakdown of communication between the two strikers. 'Van Hooijdonk's partnership with Freedman was less Butch Cassidy and the Sundance Kid and more Jack and Vera Duckworth,' said reporter Alyson Rudd.

Some players are natural communicators and leaders on the pitch. Others take a more reserved perspective. 'Paul McGrath was very quiet. He didn't talk a lot on the pitch and without communication it's impossible to set an offside trap,' said Andy Gray of Aston Villa.

Effective communication is all about the transfer of meaning, the conveying of information in a clear and uncluttered way:

'That's the ball. Keep it. Play with it. Treasure it. Look after it, and if you do, it will come back to you. The most you ever do is lend it to somebody else.' (Brian Clough, with a typical team talk)

'You can't avoid the truth. Can't make it look any better than it is. Only one thing to be said: we're in the shit.' (Brian Clough, as Norwich City beat Nottingham Forest 3–0)

'Brian Clough's secret was his ability to turn tactical complexities and instructions into a very simple message for his players.' (Ron Atkinson)

'I have tried to cut through some of the claptrap managers use and avoid the clichés.' (John Gregory, Aston Villa)

'I do not believe in formations, rather in the systems you need to make those formations work … this is all about communicating with players. You must make them understand what you're after.' (John Barnes, on arriving at Celtic)

Managers, of course, have different styles of communicating their wishes. Some rant and rave, gesticulate like madmen nearing meltdown, whilst others take a more considered and calm approach. Perhaps the best communicators are those who impart information in different ways depending on the situation or the make-up of particular players. Alex Ferguson made this point, saying, 'I'm careful which players I lay into. Some really can't handle it. Some can't even handle a team talk. There are some I don't look in the eye during a team talk because I know I am putting them under pressure.'

Those who tend to bawl out players:

'He [George Graham] bullied me a lot and I am a player that sometimes needs to be bullied and shouted at.'
(Jimmy Floyd Hasselbaink, Leeds United)

'The gaffer [Martin O'Neill] really rips into you; he's better with words than we all are, and he loves to take the piss…

You've seen him on the touch-line. He's on at us all non-stop.' (Emile Heskey)

'I don't suppose I will ever be Mr Valium.' (Gordon Strachan, Coventry City, on his touch-line rantings)

'What I said to them at half-time would be unprintable on radio.' (Gerry Francis)

'I played for Tommy Doc at Chelsea and the main thing I remember about him was that he was always throwing things. Anything from olives to pork pies.' (Ron 'Chopper' Harris, inadvertently revealing the quality of the half-time savouries down at Stamford Bridge)

'A b....cking is a b....cking in any language. When the veins start to stick out on your neck, they know what you mean.' Danny Wilson, finding a way through to the foreign players in his Sheffield Wednesday squad)

'Shouting your head off and waving arms in the air doesn't seem to have the same effect – but that's management for you.' (Stuart Pearce, as player-manager at Nottingham Forest)

Those managers who have changed tack:

'In the old days I would play holy shit with players who got things wrong. Now I can't see the point of giving myself a heart attack over other people's incompetence.' (Terry Yorath)

'You can't give them the stick you used to give them now, or take the mickey. They're a bit precious nowadays.' (Jim Smith, Derby County)

Those who take a more considered approach:

'Arsène Wenger is always calm and composed ... It just goes to show that players don't have to be approached with a whip and a chair.' (Ian Wright)

'I don't rant and rave and I don't try to be their friend either.' (Alan Curbishley, Charlton Athletic)

'That ranting and raving stuff goes in one ear and out of the other. If you talk to people they'll listen.' (Ray Wilkins)

Criticism vents feelings, but tends to be ineffective in changing the way players do things. Players with an ounce of grey matter instinctively know when they have made a mistake. Telling them adds little. A screaming bollocking only focuses on the negative and on what the player should not do. Most players need the opposite – encouragement and a focus on what they should be doing.

Breaks in play offer the coach a far more realistic chance of imparting their messages effectively. Half-time is an opportunity to change things around or refocus players in terms of the intended goal. Famous half-time and extra-time messages include:

'The Swedes can't beat us. The only ones who can beat us now are ourselves. Let's not try to do it.' (Feola, Brazil's coach, as they lead 2–1 against Sweden in the 1958 World Cup Final)

'You've won the World Cup once. Now go out and win it again. Look at the Germans. They're flat out down on the grass. They can't live with you. Not for another half hour. Not through extra time.' (Alf Ramsey)

The potential for misinterpretation is enormous, particularly with the growing diversity of languages within teams:

'At the beginning it was difficult understanding the cockneys and Scots. I ask them, "Do you speak English?"' (Ruud Gullit at Chelsea)

'We've signed five foreigners over the summer, but I'll be on hand to learn them a bit of English.' (Dennis Wise, at his most eloquent)

'For every foreigner, I would say learn the language – unless you come to Chelsea perhaps.' (Dan Petrescu, offering an alternative perspective)

'They have obviously gone for continuity because Chelsea's players can only understand broken English.' (Jim Smith, on Gianluca Vialli's appointment to succeed Ruud Gullit as boss of Chelsea)

'Jan Stejskal only knows three words of English: "my ball", "away" and one other.' (Ray Wilkins)

'I had a long chat with [Samassi Abou] before the game. He didn't understand a word.' (Harry Redknapp, West Ham United)

'I thought my team talk must have lost something in translation when we were a goal down in under a minute.' (Attilo Lombardo, briefly taking over at Crystal Palace)

'I now speak Scottish with a little bit of English.' (Jorge Cadete at Celtic)

'I studied English at school for three years but it's not the English they speak in Scotland. I had to learn a different language and even now Ian Durrant is still too difficult for me.' (Jorg Albertz at Rangers)

'I would have loved to have gone and worked with one of the top European clubs, but unfortunately I'm crap at languages.' (Dave Bassett, Nottingham Forest)

'I've been here for four years, but there still seems to be those who can't understand a word I say.' (Danny 'sithee, na then lad' Williams, a Yorkshireman, struggling to make himself understood at Swindon Town)

And also in the way messages are ultimately reported in the media:

'I have told my players never to believe what I say about them in the papers.' (Graham Taylor at Aston Villa)

Communication breaks down completely when the participants seem intent on refusing to take the other's perspective:

'Alex Totten [Kilmarnock manager] sent me to Coventry for so long I thought I'd signed for them.' (Andy Millen)

'Sometimes I do not know what is happening between me and my manager [Ruud Gullit]. I'm only 75% happy.' (Gianluca Vialli, finding the rota system at Chelsea an abhorrent brainchild of a man he couldn't trust)

'We haven't fallen out. You can't fall out with somebody you never talk to.' (Kevin Keegan, on his relationship with Sir John Hall at Newcastle United)

Professional talk or communication with psychotherapists or counsellors seeks to moderate, offer a fresh perspective and heal:

'Counselling's like having a sauna; you come out feeling
  fresh.' (Ian Wright)
'Short, back and sides please.' (Ray Parlour to Eileen Drewery,
  England's faith healer under the Glenn Hoddle regime)

In the heat of the moment and under pressure, our efforts to remain comprehensible may rapidly deteriorate. Some of the nonsense, gibberish, twaddle and eyewash emerging from the mouths of managers, players and commentators infamously includes:

'I don't think they're as good as they are.' (Kevin Keegan)
'Being given chances – and not taking them. That's what life
  is about.' (Ron Greenwood)
'I know we had home advantage, which does give you an
  advantage. But nothing to be feared though.' (Bobby
  Robson)
'The margin is very marginal.' (Bobby Robson)
'I'll tell you what, zero – zero's a big score.' (The big man
  himself, Ron Atkinson)
'I would also think that the action-replay showed it to be
  worse than it actually was, Brian.' (Ron Atkinson again)
'Strangely, in slow-motion replay, the ball seemed to hang in
  the air for even longer.' (David Acfield)
'There was a paradox of air in the town when we arrived in
  Watford this afternoon.' (Andy Smith)
'Well, we could have had a penalty there to save us from
  penalties.' (John Motson)
'It's been a first half in keeping with the whole of the match.'
  (Martin Tyler)
'It's been a night of frustration. United can't find an end to
  the cul-de-sac.' (Alan Parry)
'He's marked his entrance with an error of some
  momentum.' (Barry Davies)
'You must be strong in March when the fish are down.'
  (Gianluca Vialli)

'And Whiteside philosophically makes his way to the far post.' (Martin Tyler)

'They're still only 1–0 down – if there's such a thing as only 1–0 down against Brazil.' (Alan Parry)

'Chesterfield 1, Chester 1. Another score draw there in the local derby.' (Des Lynam)

'Ian Durrant has grown both physically and metaphorically in the close season.' (Jock Wallace)

'We didn't think we'd come here tonight and get any sort of result.' (Les Sealey)

'Outside of quality, we had other qualities.' (Bertie Mee)

'There's Kevin Reeves, who's just turned 22, and proving an ill wind blows nobody any good.' (David Coleman)

'I'm afraid that Francis this season has been suffering from a panacea of injury.' (Dale Barnes)

'The acoustics seem to get louder.' (Hugh Johns)

'Seven games we've lost 1–0, another seven we've drawn 0–0. If we'd drawn the 1–0 games we lost, we'd have another seven points. If the seven goalless draws had been 1–0 to us, we would have 28 points more and be third in the Premiership.' (Alan Smith, Crystal Palace, fighting relegation, unsuccessfully)

Stating the patently obvious is an old trick designed to avoid an uncomfortable question. However, it would be hazardous to guess the origins of the following comments, which have a discernible hint of the obvious about them:

'The World Cup – truly an international event.' (John Motson)

'Football's football: if that weren't the case it wouldn't be the game that it is.' (Garth Crooks)

'We don't always get from slow motion the pace at which they play.' (John Barrett)

'Newcastle, of course, unbeaten in their last five wins.' (Brian Moore)

'Believe it or not, goals can change a game.' (Mick Channon)

'The goals made such a difference to the way this game went.' (John Motson)

'If you're only going to score your sort of one goal or less,
   you're not going to get your victories.' (Trevor Brooking)
'Brooking trying one of those impossible crosses, which on
   that occasion was impossible.' (Brian Moore)
'Dalglish – he's the sort of player who's so unique.'
   (Bob Wilson)
'There's never been a good time to score an own goal
   against yourself.' (John Greig)
'And with just four minutes gone, the score is already 0–0.'
   (Ian Dark)
'Liverpool are ahead 2–1. It couldn't be a closer lead.'
   (Peter Jones)
'Mills is just Mickey Mills and has been since year dot.'
   (Bobby Robson)
'He has a great understanding of where the goalkeeper is in
   relation to the goal.' (David Pleat)
'So different from the scenes in 1872, at the Cup Final that
   none of us can remember.' (John Motson)
'It's a renaissance – or, put more simply, some you win, some
   you lose.' (Des Lynam)
'You can't really call yourselves giant-killers any more, as
   you kill giants so often.' (Bryon Butler)

A contradiction is also a familiar way of perplexing an audience:

'The Bulgarians are going forward, more in hope than in
   optimism.'
'We are now into the third and final quarter of this game.'
   (Irish commentator)
'I think that was a moment of cool panic there …' (Ron
   Atkinson)
'Platt – singularly in two minds.' (John Motson)
'McCarthy shakes his head in agreement with the referee.'
   (Martin Tyler)
'George Graham will be happy with a draw – I know how
   ambitious and positive he is.' (Terry Neill)
'Everything in our favour was against us.' (Danny
   Blanchflower)

'With the last kick of the game, Bobby McDonald scored with a header.' (Alan Parry)

'You've got to miss them to score sometimes.' (Dave Bassett)

'The score line really didn't reflect the outcome.' (Tony Gubba)

'The only thing Norwich didn't get was the goal that they finally got.' (Jimmy Greaves)

'It really needed the blink of an eyelid, otherwise you would have missed it.' (Peter Jones)

'They've got their feet on the ground and if they stay that way they'll go places.' (John Gidman)

'He put it just where he meant it and it passed the Luxembourg goalpost by 18 inches.' (Bryon Butler)

'Kicked wide of the goal with such precision.' (Des Lynam)

'Albion face their stiffest task yet in the freezing hothouse at Sunderland.' (Malcolm Boyden)

'I'm not superstitious or anything like that, but I'll just hope we'll play our best and put it in the lap of the gods.' (Terry Neill)

'Exeter 3, Swindon 4 – a good tight defensive game there.' (Bryon Butler)

Ian Rush: 'Deadly ten times out of ten. But that wasn't one of them.' (Peter Jones)

'Williams beat Shilton from 35 yards ... and you don't beat Shilton from 35 yards.' (Peter Jones)

'The goals from Carrow Road, where the game ended 0–0.' (Elton Welsby)

'You can't get any bigger than the quarter-finals of the FA Cup.' (Alex Ferguson)

'You couldn't have counted the number of moves Alan Ball made ... I counted four and possibly five.' (John Motson)

'The Spaniards have been reduced to aiming aimless balls into the box.' (Ron Atkinson)

'Northern Ireland have had several chances and haven't scored but England had no chances and scored twice.' (Trevor Brooking)

'History is all about todays and not about yesterdays.' (Brian Moore)

'There aren't many last chances left for him.' (Archie
  MacPherson)
'All the team are 100% behind the manager, but I can't speak
  for the rest of the squad.' (Brian Greenhoff)
'Without picking out anyone in particular, I thought Mark
  Wright was tremendous.' (Graeme Souness)
'The better team drew.' (Andy King, Mansfield Town)

And then there is the improbable:

'He put his body between himself and the defender.'
  (Paul Sturrock, hinting at depersonalisation)
'I'm a forgotten man in Bobby Robson's mind.'
  (Glenn Hoddle)
'Gullit ... turned to find he had someone standing on his
  toes.' (John Motson)
'In the past we used to think that keepers grew on trees and
  maybe in a way they did.' (Ray Clemence, goalkeeping
  coach and part-time landscape gardener)
'What it does, Brian, is make an impossible job harder.' (Ron
  Atkinson)
'Bergkamp's going to empty the hole.' (Andy Gray)
'Chris Waddle is off the field at the moment; exactly the
  position he is at his most menacing.' (Gerald Sinstadt)
'If that was a penalty, I'll plait sawdust.' (Ron Atkinson)
'West Ham ... like actors playing to an empty stage.' (Bryon
  Butler)

An unfortunate turn of phrase is always a good one:

'I wouldn't mind being a fly on Larry Lloyd's shorts.' (Martin
  Johnson)
'Southall's goal kick breaks off Venison's head.' (Clive
  Tyldesley)
'That's Robson – a totally convicted player.' (Jimmy
  Armfield)
'I can't see us getting beat now – once we get our tails in
  front.' (Jim Platt)

Communication tells us about the communicator – the style and metaphors are an expression of the communicator's psyche. Some mixed and dodgy metaphors:

'No one hands you cups on a plate.' (Terry McDermott)

'Omens are there to be broken.' (Bob Wilson)

'We are on the crest of a slump.' (Tommy Docherty)

'I'm on top of the moon.' (Lee Hendrie, Aston Villa, on his England call-up)

'You could cut the atmosphere with a knife, it was so electric.' (Brian Marjoribanks)

'In a nutshell we were murdered.' (Ron Atkinson of Nottingham Forest, after a humiliating 8–1 trouncing)

'We could be putting the hammer in Luton's coffin.' (Ray Wilkins)

'And Keegan there like a surgeon's knife – bang.' (Bryon Butler)

'The world is your lobster.' (Mark Lawrenson, as Oxford United gain promotion)

'Rangers are really exerting the screw now.' (Archie McPherson)

'He had two stabs at the cherry.' (Alan Green)

'That one sold Wilkins a lot of trouble, giving Mortimer an easy bite of the ball.' (Hugh Johns)

'Pat Jennings clapped his hands round the ball like banging a piece of toast.' (Barry Davies)

'They can crumble as easily as ice-cream in this heat.' (Sammy Nelson)

'Beckenbauer really has gambled all his eggs.' (Ron Atkinson)

'He went down like a sack of potatoes, then made a meal of it.' (Trevor Brooking)

'The proof of the pudding is in the eating and Villa aren't pulling up any trees.' (Tony Butler)

'I don't hold water with that theory.' (Ron Greenwood)

'Houghton got up like a tree blown down in a storm.' (Peter Jones)

'Obviously for Scunthorpe it would be a nice scalp to put Wimbledon on their bottoms.' (Dave Bassett)

'It was a bit like a game of chess; they kicked the ball from one end to the other.' (John Mone)

'The Arsenal defence is skating close to the wind.' (Jack Charlton)

'Butcher goes forward as Ipswich throw their last trump card into the fire.' (Bryan Butler)

'I have other irons in the fire, but I'm keeping them close to my chest.' (John Bond)

'He hit that one like an arrow.' (Alan Parry)

'Tottenham haven't thrown in the towel even though they've been under the gun.' (Bobby Charlton)

'It's as if there's a laser beam in his chest attracting the ball.' (Jimmy Hill)

'Ian Baird is dashing around like a steam roller up front.' (Martin Tyler)

'It was that game that put the Everton ship back on the road.' (Alan Green)

'Celtic were at one time nine points ahead, but somewhere along the road, their ship went off the rails.' (Richard Park)

'He's got a left foot, and left foots are like bricks of gold.' (Jimmy Greaves)

'Fine tackling by Butcher using his telescopic legs.' (Jock Brown)

'They've missed so many chances they must be wringing their heads in shame.' (Ron Greenwood)

'And Bailey comes out to save. Immediately there is a whole wasps' nest of blue shirts swarming round him.' (Bryon Butler)

'Sporting Lisbon in their green and white hooped shirts … like a team of zebras.' (Peter Jones)

'Again Mariner and Butcher are trying to work the oracle on the near post.' (Martin Tyler)

Chapter 17

Team spirit

'The team spirit became as good as a goal to us.'
Jack Charlton, Leeds United

The power of team spirit has become a cliché. Everyone now recognises its importance. When teams of supposedly inferior quality are galvanised by their team spirit, more than occasionally they will upset the odds. Team spirit is unquestionably what underdogs are made of. It is, however, also what champions are made of.

Team spirit can be construed in three ways. It is a sense of togetherness generated by members of the team pulling their weight and collectively striving to meet an agreed goal. Achieving a clean sheet away from home requires everyone to fully work at their role. Secondly, it demands altruism: being prepared to help each other out, to cover for team-mates, to support others when things get tough. 'There's a great team spirit in the Forest team. You know everybody's going to be fighting for each other. You know you're not going to get shat on by your mate who's going to think, "I'll get out of a tackle" or whatever,' said Steve Stone of Nottingham Forest to illustrate this point.

Finally, team strength derives from a respect for each other:

'A team really only needs respect for each other rather than affection to be successful.' (Tony Adams)
'Alan Shearer's a lads' lad. It's more important for him to be accepted by all the lads than to receive all the accolades that have come his way.' (Mike Newell)
'Before the game I asked my team-mates that whoever scored the first goal would raise his shirt. We wanted to show him

we are really close to him.' (Gianfranco Zola, dedicating his
goal to No. 10, Pierluigi Casiraghi, badly injured in the
previous game)

When teams gel and work for others there is a gestalt – a sense
that the whole is greater than the sum of its parts. This generates
high morale and spirit within the camp. Harry Redknapp, at West
Ham United, had an interesting way of describing the degree of
team spirit: 'That is exactly the sort of spirit you need at a club.
You don't see it much any more these days, but we've got it in
spades here.'

Team spirit should run through, not just the first team, but the
whole club. This point is well illustrated by Rodney Marsh, who
said, 'All a manager has to do is keep eleven players happy – the
eleven in the reserves. The first team are happy because they're in
the first team.' Developing team spirit appears to be an important
task for the manager, and one that severely tests his skills. As Peter
Reid at Sunderland commented, 'There's a tremendous team spirit
and character and you can't buy that on the transfer market.'

Team spirit develops in the dressing room, in training and on the
field, but rarely in the bars, night-clubs and snooker halls that
players might frequent. Gordon Strachan made this point when he
said, 'Team spirit is not a commodity which comes cheap, and it is
not something you build with boozy nights out together but from
what players do for each other on the field.' Criticism can gel a
team, if it draws strength from adversity. Bad press, a belief that
everyone's against them, or opposition that slates the team, can
unite the team to fight a joint cause and prove the critics wrong.
'The universal dislike of the team [Revie's Leeds United] made
them even stronger as a unit,' noted Lee Chapman. The moral is,
slag off the opposition at your peril.

Dressing rooms are a cauldron of banter and ridicule. They
provide a barometer of team spirit where players swear their
allegiance to the cause. 'Professional footballers are among the
sharpest group of people you'll ever meet, and the banter,
comments, the slickness of the wind-up and the psychological
torturing that goes on is both witty and intelligent,' said Pat
Nevin. Some of the jolly japes include:

'I have teamed up with [Ian] Wrighty and we have great fun. He cuts up my underwear and I cut up his socks and we always blame someone else.' (Glen Helder, on those heady days at Arsenal)

'You walk in and someone's nailed your shoes to the floor and you're like "Oh, here we go again."' (Neil Sullivan, Wimbledon)

'I put a fish in Aaron Winter's car, underneath the seat, and it stank for a week – he didn't know where it was. It's very important to me, to enjoy my football.' (Paul Ince)

'When [Steve] Sedgley had gone out for training I got one of his squash socks and had a shit in it. I was careful not to do too much otherwise he'd have noticed the weight. So after training he went to put the sock on, rolled it up and put his thumbs straight in my shit.' (David Speedie at Coventry City)

'Luca Vialli's humour is very dry. During training, just as someone is about to run, he will pull their shorts down to their knees so they can't move.' (Mark Nicholls, Chelsea)

'You give a few sticks and you get a few sticks, but you always give Jonathan Gould a few extra sticks … but it is only friendly kind of sticks. That's the way it is.' (Henrik Larsson, Celtic)

'We slaughtered each other in the dressing room beforehand. There was no way Wimbledon were going to let anyone feast on our carcass after that.' (Vinnie Jones)

'Chris Hay is the most likeable lad in the Swindon dressing room, so to make him feel at home we spend all our time taking the mickey out of him.' (Mark Walters)

Stuart Ripley, who has visited a few dressing rooms in his time, has a more unusual recipe for developing team spirit. He said, 'I know its not very professional, players falling around with beer in them, but it does the lads good … I've never been to a club yet that hasn't had a few good fights: it's good for team spirit.'

Team spirit is vulnerable. Infighting, dissent in the camp and simmering feuds are distinct signs of a team in trouble:

'It wouldn't be a major tournament if there wasn't talk of rows and disagreements in the Dutch camp.' (Ruud Gullit)

'There's a rat in the camp trying to throw a spanner in the works.' (Chris Cattlin)

'He [Marc Overmars] plays only for himself and will never give me a ball I can score from. There is no reason I should stay quiet and run like a dog behind missiles he sends my way.' (Nicolas Anelka)

'I don't mind playing football with him [Hristo Stoichkov] on the pitch but I never want to see him outside the ground.' (Ronald Koeman)

'Some players were like a cancer in the dressing room. If they weren't in the side, they would stir shit.' (Tommy Docherty, on his time at Manchester United)

'The most minute of errors puncture their [Spurs'] paper-thin confidence, they argue and remonstrate like spoilt little rich kids. Collective and individual responsibility is non-existent.' (Russell Kempson)

'Bobby [Charlton] and I were plying our talents in a waste-land. I felt that no matter what I produced there was no end product. Bobby felt the same and neither of us were very tolerant of the lesser players.' (George Best)

'I'm not prepared to let my career go down the pan. Right now this team [Forest] is not good enough to survive in the Premiership.' (Pierrre van Hooijdonk, putting the boot in)

'Whether the other players want to share in his celebrations does not bother me … I do not think that it will bother Pierre if he is shunned when he scores. He dropped us in it at the start of the season.' (Dave Bassett, on why Pierre van Hooijdonk was cold shouldered, after returning to Nottingham Forest following his self-imposed exile in Holland. After his first goal on his return to the side, few team-mates shared in the celebrations)

Nicknames are a common bonding practice. They signal acceptance within the team. Sometimes, however, the sobriquet can prove a player's undoing:

'Paul Ince wants everyone to call him Guvnor, but we call him Incey.' (Lee Sharpe)

'One day Les Sealey announced he wanted to be known as "the cat". We'd be playing a match and you'd hear "the cat's ball" and Les would come for it. But he didn't always get there, so Mick Harford christened him "Tiddles".' (Steve Foster)

'I haven't got a nickname. I just get called all sorts of stuff. But they're not really nicknames – they're just abusive.' (Frank Sinclair at Chelsea)

'Kimble's left foot is known as the wand, but there was nothing magical about that pass.' (Andy Gray, on the Wimbledon full back)

Some nicknames of note from past and present:

In the net

'H' (David Seaman, because of his Hands)
'Tarzan' (Peter Shilton)
'The Cat' (Tim Flowers)
'The Flying Pig' (Tommy Lawrence, Liverpool goalkeeper)
'The Clown' (Bruce Grobbelaar)
'Lurch' (Dave Beasant)
'The Black Spider' (Lev Yashin)
'The Black Octopus' (Lev Yashin)

Sweeping

'The Kaiser' (Franz Beckenbauer)

At the back

'The Black Pearl' (Paul McGrath)
'Gentle Giant' (Jack Charlton)
'Giraffe' (Jack Charlton)
'Crazy Horse' (Emlyn Hughes)
'The Horse' (Oleg Luzhny)

'Psycho' (Stuart Pearce)
'The Anfield Iron' (Tommy Smith)
Ron 'Chopper' Harris
Norman 'Bites Yer Legs' Hunter
Harry 'The Dog' Cripps
Neil 'Razor' Ruddock
'Hello, My name is Satan' (Slogan on Julian Dicks' t-shirt)
'Rodders' (Tony Adams, after the character in *Only Fools and Horses*)
'Rash' (Chris Perry, because he is all over his opponent)
'Iron Mike' (Duberry, because of his close resemblance to Tyson)
'The Beast of Bilbao' (Andoni Goicoechea after breaking Maradona's leg)

The wing back

'Berge' (Graeme Le Saux)
'Five Bellies' (Kenny Sansom)
'Wing Nut' (Justin Edinburgh)
Johnny 'Budgie' Byrne (because he never stopped talking)
'The Dog' (Warren Barton because 'he arrives at training in shirt, trousers and shoes. And his hair is lovely. We call him "The Dog", as in "the dog's bollocks".' (Robert Lee))

The midfield engine room

'Dogshit' (Remi Moses)
'The Ferret' (Ray Houghton)
'The Rat' (Dennis Wise)
'Suitcase' (Gary Megson, because he never stayed long at any club)
Roy 'Damien' Keane (after the character in *The Omen*)
'Nijinsky' (Colin Bell, because he never stopped running)
'Faxe' (John Jensen, after a Danish beer)
'El Bandito' (Nobby Stiles)
'Manu' (Emmanuel Petit)

'Pitbull' (Edgar Davids)
'Piranha' (Edgar Davids)

The creative link

'Le God' (Matthew Le Tissier)
Marcus 'Gravy' Browning
'Chippy' (Liam Brady)
'Pedro' (Peter Beardsley)
'Quasimodo' (Peter Beardsley)
Ray 'Butch' Wilkins
'Il Divino' (Falcao)
'The Leper' (Steven Hughes, because he's always on the
  sidelines)
'Chippy' (Ian Crook)
'Rambo' (Jan Molby)

The wide men

'Digger' (John Barnes)
'Shaggy' (Darren Anderton)
'Sicknote' (Darren Anderton)
'Merlin the Magician' (Chris Waddle)
'El Magnifico' (David Ginola)
'Little Bird' (Garrincha)
'The Moose' (Kevin Gallagher)
'Lino' (Chris Kiwomya, because he used to lie around in
  training)
'Big Bamber' (Steve Heighway, because of his university
  background)
'Little Bamber' (Brian Hall)

The strikers

'The Cobra' (Romario, because of his deadly strike)
'The Vulture' (Emilio Butragueno)
'Der Bomber' (Gerd Muller)
'Snowy' (Noel Whelan)

'Smudger' (Alan Smith)

'Bonnie' (Clyde Wijnhard)

'The Helicopter' (Ivan Zamorano, because of his ability to hover at the far post)

'The Toxteth Terror' (Robbie Fowler)

Ole 'Baby Face Assassin' Solsjkaer

'Jaws' (Joe Jordan)

'Big Chief' (Wayne Allison)

'Satchmo' (Ian Wright)

'Il Divino' (Roberto Baggio)

Kenny 'Les' Dalglish (after he wrongly named a member of staff)

'Dudley' (Ally McCoist, after his manager, Graeme Souness, called him an effing dud)

'Golden Bollocks' (Ally McCoist)

'Golden Bollocks' (Gary Lineker)

'Sparky' (Mark Hughes)

Bryan 'Pop' Robson

'Mister Angry' (Mike Newell)

'Tosh' (Ian Rush)

'Juke Box' (Gordon Durie)

'Albert Tatlock' (Paul Warhurst)

'Sniffer' (Alan Clarke)

'Trigger' (Chris Sutton)

'The Back Panther' (Eusebio)

'Rocket' (Ronnie Rosenthal, because 'the ball usually ends up in orbit after he's struck it' (Paul Simpson and Ray Spiller))

'The Volcano' (Paolo Di Canio)

'Sukerman' (Davor Suker)

Jimmy 'The Tree' Quinn

'Supermac' (Malcolm McDonald)

'The Divine Ponytail' (Roberto Baggio)

'Sir Les' (Les Ferdinand)

'El Camion (The Truck)' (Gabriel Batistuta)

'The White Feather' (Fabrizio Ravanelli)

'Raging Bull' (Hristo Stoichkov)

'The Genius' (Dejan Savicervic)

'The White Pelé' (Zico)
'Grumpy' (Frank Stapleton)
'The Little Cannon' (Ferenc Puskas)

'We've got complete harmonium in the dressing room.'
  (Joe Smith, Blackpool, 1950s)

Chapter 18

Fair and foul play

'Nobby Stiles: an assassin; brutal; badly intentioned and a bad sportsman.'
Otto Gloria, Benfica manager, not afraid to mince words or apply a verbal hammering

'The talk among your fellow professionals is that you are steadily becoming a dirty, nasty, bastard.'
John Fashanu of Eric Cantona

Soccer, we are endlessly reminded, is a man's game. Contact is endemic, and without it the game would deteriorate into a convivially gay farce. A bone-shaking tackle to win the ball, the jostling for space at a corner and shoulder wrestling in the chase for a ball remain appropriate within the laws of the game. Late tackles from behind, shirt pulling and mounting the centre-forward to win a header are generally pulled up by the competent referee, but nevertheless have become an intrinsic and character-istic part of the modern game.

What crosses the thin line between acceptability and illegality is the cynical, reckless, undisciplined challenge. A thigh-high two-footed jump tackle from behind or raking the studs down the back of an opponent's calf at a corner, go well beyond the acceptable face of fair contact.

Those who have few qualms about going for the leg, throat and other delicate regions rather than the ball include:

'I'd kick my own brother if necessary.' (Steve McMahon)
'Terry Paine would kick his own mother.' (Mick Channon)

'I didn't try to break his leg. I only tried to kick him.'
  (Roy Keane, implying a bit of boot is OK then)
'This is not a dancing academy.' (Claudio Gentile)
'Vinnie Jones is a player who regards it as a matter of
  personal honour to intimidate the nation's finest, to
  castrate them with a shattering late tackle early in the game,
  to rip their ears off and spit in the hole.' (Jasper Rees)
'Marco Tardelli's been responsible for more scar tissue than
  the surgeons of Harefield Hospital.' (Jimmy Greaves)
'Tommy Smith could start a riot in a graveyard.'
  (Bill Shankly)
'If Ron "Chopper" Harris was in a good mood, he'd put
  iodine on his studs before a game.' (Jimmy Greaves)
'I don't mind if we pick up a few yellow cards. I'm looking
  for a team which fights. No more nicey-nicey football.'
  (Steve McMahon)
'Harry Cripps's various achievements with the club
  [Millwall] included breaking more legs than any other
  player in the history of the league.' (David Pickering)
'We will come back kicking and fighting like English teams
  always have.' (Stuart Pearce, after England lose to Italy)
'Dennis Bergkamp is such a nice man, such a tremendous
  gentleman – it's going to be very hard for me to kick him.'
  (Tony Adams, as he faces up to his team-mate playing for
  Holland)
'It's strange for me to respect a manager who, every previous
  time we have met, has stuck his studs in my jock-strap.'
  (Ray Wilkins, on Graeme Souness, his new manager at
  Rangers)
'Graeme Souness is the hardest, most ruthless player I
  have come up against in 15 years of top class football …
  He isn't just hard. There is definitely a nasty side to him.'
  (Frank Worthington)
'If it had been a reckless challenge I would have showed my
  studs.' (Vinnie Jones, following a sending off for clashing
  with Ruud Gullit)
'Emerson's a typical Brazilian … a big strong lad who's not
  afraid to put his foot in.' (Neil Cox)

'Craig Short clattered Ruud Gullit with a tackle that was late, high and ugly.' (David Prentice)

'I think he [Romanian defender Mihai Mocanu] must have created a new tackle. For the general impression was that he started kicking at knee level, and worked up to the throat.' (Francis Lee)

'Juninho's so tiny. I half expected him to come out with a school satchel on his back. If he had, I'd have trodden on his packed lunch.' (Andy Thorn)

'Bobby Collins was a genuine artist on the ball, but he could slice your leg off at the knee and take the bottom bit home before you knew anything about it.' (Jim Baxter)

'Mike Summerbee was very hard, very aggressive and very skilful. If he couldn't give the full back a chasing he used to give him a clobbering.' (Francis Lee)

'There was only one way to play against Frank [Worthington]. Kick him as soon as you can.' (Paddy Crerand)

'Tommy Smith thought he was having a bad game unless he had clattered someone across the knees.' (Tommy Docherty)

'Terry Paine had a knack of getting up everyone's nose. He had a terrible reputation for going over the top in the tackle and kicking people.' (Mick Channon)

'I went in for the ball and never ever touched Ted McMinn. And he went three or four feet up in the air.' (Julian Dicks, explaining his third sending off in four months)

'Graeme Souness clearly aimed to get the pecking order laid down before any real nonsense blew up. It was like the law of the jungle.' (Mark Hughes)

'Basically I'm a nasty little guy because I always like to win. If I have to boot someone, I'll boot them: simple as that.' (Dennis Wise)

'Hartson's got more previous than Jack the Ripper.' (Harry Redknapp, after Hartson's dismissal against Derby County for West Ham United)

And the result, from the recipient's perspective:

'Every English player autographed my leg with his studs.'
   (Gunther Netzer)
'It's the first time, after a match, that we've had to replace
   divots in the players.' (Ron Atkinson)
'We have been eliminated brutally – I would say, scientific-
   ally.' (Michel Hildago of France, following their defeat by
   West Germany in the 1982 World Cup semi-final after
   Harold Schumacher half killed Patrick Battiston when he
   was through and about to score to seal victory. Schumacher
   did not receive even a mild ticking off)

The elbow is a particularly appalling means of maiming an
opponent. As Mark Lawrenson put it, 'The use of the elbow is the
worst crime in soccer. People talk of over the top tackles but at
least you've got a chance, albeit a small one, to save yourself as the
boot comes in. The elbow is a heinous crime, used by the lowest of
the low. It's virtually impossible to protect yourself against it.'

'I can recall elbowing Trevor Stevens in the face by the
   dug-out. The crowd loved it and it made me feel part of the
   club.' (Julian Dicks)
'I just knew I was going to elbow him [Franz Carr] … I had it
   in my mind that I was going to elbow him and that was it –
   bang.' (Julian Dicks again)

And, again, the crushed words of a recipient after an elbow:

'When I saw my face, I felt like the Elephant Man. This is not
   a normal injury. Fashanu was playing without due care and
   attention.' (Gary Mabbutt, with a fractured skull after
   tangling with Fashanu's elbow)

In-your-face dissent and foul language are likely to upset the
referee more than the delicate disposition of other players:

'When a player says "shit" as he trips over the ball, it does
   not usually mean that he has slipped on a dog poop.' (The
   Bishop of Haslingden, former referee)

'In those days you could say what you wanted to refs,
provided they never heard it.' (Francis Lee)

'I've been called a firebrand, a hooligan, a thug, a dirty player
… it's the absolute truth that talking out of turn has been the
cause of most of the 15 bookings I've had.' (Billy Bremner)

'I swore at referees throughout my first season with
Tottingham, but they never booked me because I swore in
Spanish.' (Ossie Ardiles)

'I do swear a lot but the advantage is that having played
abroad, I can choose a different language from the
referee's.' (Jurgen Klinsmann)

'I verbally abused referees down the years, but this was
simply because I always felt they were on a different planet
to the players. We always felt completely misunderstood.'
(Tommy Smith)

'He probably doubted his parentage with words of anglo-
saxon.' (Mark Lawrenson, explaining the dismissal of Phil
Stamp of Middlesbrough)

'He'll come towards you aggressively, with his face twisted in
rage, giving you a load of verbals.' (Brian Hill, referee, on
Alan Shearer)

'My dad always told me to keep my mouth shut. Now I've
realised I've reached the stage where I must learn not to do
it in big tournaments. I know I'll never be sent off for
England.' (A prophetic David Beckham before the 1998
World Cup)

'I've been punished for striking a goalkeeper, for spitting at
supporters, for throwing my shirt at a referee, for calling
my manager a bag of shit. I called those who judged a
bunch of idiots.' (That meek-mannered wallflower, Eric
Cantona)

Seeking to influence the referee's decisions by hassling him,
inciting him to send someone off or hounding his personal space is
an insidious and devious development:

'What made me angry was the reaction of the Southampton
players. They surrounded the referee and were shouting at

him to send me off. I couldn't believe fellow professionals
would do that.' (Terry Butcher)

'Neil Ruddock would run 15 or 20 yards to an incident that
had nothing to do with him.' (Jimmy Case)

'Some are trying to con refs into awarding penalties and free
kicks, as well as get opponents a yellow or red card.' (Hugh
Williamson, referee)

'All the Argentinians swarmed around him – most of all
Maradona.' (Brian Moore, during the infamous 1990
World Cup Final)

'The most frequent accusation against Bremner was that he
tried to referee matches. That was rubbish ... sure he
yapped away all the time and he challenged decisions you
made but never in a way which you could send him off for.'
(Pat Partridge, referee)

The sly, cynical, dirty tricks performed on the blind side of the
referee are mastered by the shifty, mordant, sneering gangster
usually playing a blinder for the other side:

'The likes of Allan Clarke at Leeds and Terry Paine of
Southampton were sly. There was always one or two
sneaky ones. They were not up front about it.' (Tommy
Smith)

'You would tackle Denis [Law] and all of a sudden it was like
a needle in the side – whack, take that one! You had gone to
make the tackle but you were the one who ended up hurt.'
(Emlyn Hughes)

'Forwards like Chelsea's Peter Osgood, Southampton's Terry
Paine, Mike Summerbee of Manchester City and most
especially, Johnny Giles of Leeds. They were hard. But they
also had skill which enabled them to get away with subtle
fouls that the referee couldn't spot.' (George Best)

'Kenny Dalglish is cute. He uses his whole body, legs, arms
and elbows and often sails on the borderline of fair play.'
(Graeme Souness)

'Betini was an artist at fouling a man without getting caught.
Whenever he came close he managed to dig me in the ribs,

or put his fist in my stomach, or kick me in the shins during a tackle.' (Pelé, on the Italian)

'We were being spat on. We were being punched when the ball was maybe 50 yards away. We were victims of vicious forearm smashes across the face when the referee and linesman were not looking. We were having our hair pulled.' (Gordon Strachan, reflecting on the Uruguayans)

'They were up to all the cynical stuff. Pulling your hair, spitting, treading on your toes.' (Andy Nelson of Ipswich, noting the Italian style)

Claudio Gentile: 'I've never come up against anyone else who has the dirty tricks off to such perfection.' (Charlie Nicholas)

'Gentile, he belied his name by firmly grasping my testicles.' (Steve Coppell)

'Gentile would do anything to upset me. He nipped me, he pulled my hair, he held my jersey – all the annoying niggly things that referees don't always pick up on; even the fans can't see what's going on.' (Charlie Nicholas)

'As the two teams walked down the tunnel at the start of the game, I felt a terrible pain on my right calf as someone kicked with brute force. I turned. It was Bobby Collins. "And that's just for starters Bestie," he said.' (George Best)

'Alan Ball kept confusing my shins with the ball.' (Jim Baxter)

Retribution and retaliation are far from cute. They mark the player as emotionally vulnerable:

'Oh, and in another match, I threw a punch at this player … but I did get sent off for that one.' (Roy Keane, in an advert splashed across the nation's magazines)

'After tonight, England v. Argentina will be remembered for what a player did with his feet.' (Another advert featuring David Beckham, who was subsequently ordered off for kicking an opponent in retribution)

'How could he [David Beckham] be so stupid? It doesn't matter whether he barely touched him: he aimed a kick at the guy and it was clearly premeditated. The referee had no choice but to send him off.' (Barry Davies, on the same incident when Beckham was dismissed for England against Argentina)

'Football is a game of skill. We kick them a bit and they kick us a bit.' (Graham Roberts)

'I'm the type of person that if someone stabs me in the back, then I would do twice as worse back to them.' (Mark Bosnich)

'Loads of people thought bad thoughts of Gilesy [Johnny Giles] and wanted to top him.' (Mick Channon)

'Retaliation is pointless and stupid because the consequences are always the long, lonely walk ... But I defy any mortal to take kick after brutal kick, then be tossed high enough in the air to catch a lift back down on the space shuttle.' (Willie Johnston)

'I challenged for the ball with Steve Williams and managed to come out on top. I passed the ball to a colleague and as I turned away, Williams reacted in a way I found hard to comprehend – whether intentional or not, he spat in my face.' (Lee Chapman)

'I put a good solid challenge in on Giles. After Giles had picked himself up and dusted himself down he just glanced at Charlton, Hunter and Bremner whilst nodding in my general direction. It was like having a contract put out on you.' (Howard Kendall)

'I cannot even remember getting in a good tackle against him [Johnny Giles] for he was quick and nippy and if there was the slightest chance of him being hurt you would suddenly be confronted by a full set of studs.' (Graeme Souness)

'I was the guy who kicked an opponent if he hurt Johnny [Haynes].' (Alan Mullery)

'Players like Peter Storey allowed their team-mates to play without fear of retribution from the opposition.' (Terry Neill)

'I always stood up for myself. That's how I was brought up. Coming from Holloway, you learn from the pram to nut people who pick on you.' (Charlie George)

'I was fairly crude in my tackling, with no finesse at all and I
admit that I did tend to go over the top in retaliation rather
than as an instigator.' (Graeme Souness)

'Nail him [Jimmy Case] just once and it never leaves your
mind that he will get you back. Given time, it's a promise
that Casey will have his revenge.' (Mark Hughes)

'Jimmy Case will destroy you with the ball as well as the
boot.' (Mark Hughes)

'I've got a little black book in which I keep all the names of all
the players I've got to get before I pack up playing.'
(Jack Charlton)

Graeme Souness: 'His arrogance and the way he strutted
around the pitch as though he owned it made players want
to bring him down a peg or two.' (Terry Butcher)

'Graeme Souness and I shared the same sort of hard man
motto if you like: if someone whacks you, you accept it, get
up and get on with the game, and wait for your chance to
whack them back.' (Steve McMahon)

'Souness was not a player to be crossed on the field – he
was the master at picking the time for retribution.'
(Steve McMahon)

'Do that one more time pal, and I'll rip your ear off and spit
in the hole.' (Vinnie Jones meets Kenny Dalglish)

'I just grabbed out behind me and got hold of his nuts. I just
squeezed to teach him a lesson for being so mouthy.'
(Vinnie Jones meets Paul Gascoigne's soft nether regions)

'Some players are just idiots and they wind you up and you
think "sod you", and you have to smack them one.' (Roy
Keane)

Some, a very few, learn a lesson:

'I have wasted so much energy racing around trying to kick
people because they had kicked me. Now I save my energy
to try and put the ball in the net.' (Mark Hughes)

Cheating and hoodwinking the officials are base actions and
generate protests from even the most stuporous supporters.

Diving and playacting are commonplace, but there are more sinister versions to which the trickster will resort:

'Me dive? Never. I always go straight for goal.'
(Jurgen Klinsmann)

'It wasn't for diving. I got booked for saying to their captain that he had a big nose.' (Robert Lee, rationalising his behaviour)

'No one can accuse me of diving, because I can't swim.'
(Dean Holdsworth)

David Ginola: 'I'm told he ran up the tunnel and dived in the bath.' (Joe Royle)

'I mistimed a tackle on Steve Williams ... it wasn't a bad tackle but he made a meal out of it and started writhing about in melodramatic style.' (Terry Butcher)

'Stoichkov does not know how to play fair. He plays for fouls by putting his shoulder in and then falling.' (Javier Clemente)

'The lad he tackled was limping at 100 mph soon afterwards.' (John Docherty, Millwall manager)

David Ginola: 'There's no doubt that he does have a tendency to make a meal of challenges.' (Mark Lawrenson)

Ginola: 'He's just thrown himself over and rolled and rolled. You don't act like that if you're hurt. You just stay down.'
(Lou Macari)

'German players have turned the dive into an art form.'
(Sepp Blatter)

'David Ginola has been criticised for diving, but that's the culture that these guys are brought up in.' (Terry Venables, being perhaps a tad xenophobic)

'Ramon Vega went down like he was dead. I thought he had broken his leg, but he only broke a tie up.' (Harry Redknapp, pouring derision on Vega's theatricals)

'I've just seen Gary Lineker shake hands with Jurgen Klinsmann – it's a wonder Klinsmann hasn't fallen down.'
(Ron Atkinson)

'You'd probably say that I was a cheat, but I'd just say "I'm a professional trying to win a game" ... whether that means hand-balling accidentally on purpose to score, or upending someone, I'd do it.' (Viv Anderson)

'The goal was scored a little bit by the hand of God.' (Diego Maradona)

Maradona: 'He bends the rules to suit himself.' (Sir Alf Ramsey)

'You'd find 20 quid tucked into your boots to not try too hard in the last game of the season. If they really went into it, they'd have to declare an amnesty.' (Malcolm Allison)

'I'd rather have Bruce Grobbelaar trying to throw a game than Dave Beasant trying to win one.' (Southampton fan)

'Gentlemen, the first thing you can do for me is to throw your medals in the dustbin because you've never won anything fairly. You've done it by cheating.' (Brian Clough, introducing himself to the Leeds players)

And the players who rise above cheating and get on with the game:

'Pelé does everything superbly with the possible exception of taking a dive in an opponent's penalty area.' (Martin Peters)

'Juninho's not one of those foreigners who rolls about when he is kicked.' (Viv Anderson)

'They serve a drink in Glasgow called a Souness – one half and you're off.' (Tommy Docherty)

Chapter 19

Having the bottle

'I prefer my players not to be too clever at other things. It means they concentrate on football.'
Bill Nicholson, Spurs manager

Footballers are, however, more than just footballers. They have lives outside the game, however clever or daft they may appear to be, to paraphrase the great Spurs manager. Even though most players would fundamentally construe themselves as an athlete or sportsman, they develop aspects of themselves that have little relevance to soccer. As most players spend only a fraction of their week in training and playing, the remaining time is free. Free for them to engage in whatever pursuits catch their fancy. How footballers conduct themselves when they leave the confines of the club is largely their own responsibility. They construct non-footballing selves. They enter different worlds with different identities. Perhaps self as an artist (à la Cantona), gardener (Mark Wright), TV talk show host (Ian Wright), film star (Vinnie Jones), erudite thinker (Graeme Le Saux), dog breeder (Julian Dicks), fisherman (Jack Charlton), golfer (Alan Hansen) or husband (Frank Le Beouf).

Interestingly, Tony Adams of Arsenal suggests he began drinking because others found it difficult to perceive of him as anything other than a footballer, a realisation that people really didn't know him. 'All my self-worth was in what I did [playing football], not what I was. All my pats on the back came from being Tony the footballer,' he said.

Much is made of being professional off the field. If a player conducts himself in a sound way in his non-footballing roles, then he is seen as being a good professional. On the other hand, players

slipping into roles that potentially affect their physical or psychological state are considered unprofessional. They are hedonists,
individuals or mavericks. They are considered unreliable and their
commitment to the cause is questioned. Gordon Taylor, PFA Chief
Executive, indicated, 'We have stressed that it isn't just about what
a player does on the training pitch and in matches. All that can be
undone if the rest of a player's life is not as it should be.'

Fabrizio Ravanelli, in his denial, demonstrated something of a
continental's view of the home footballer: 'I swear that I never
said that English players are too knackered, too overweight and
too drunk.' Frank Worthington illustrates vividly the way it was
back in the 1970s and '80s, stating that, 'As a professional
footballer you are at a loose end most afternoons of the year. You
are always on the look-out for outlets that will occupy your time
and if it's not golf then there is always the bookies or racing.'
George Best, however, presented a different slant, even if he was
somewhat unique in this respect: 'We only trained in the morning,
but instead of going off after lunch with the other lads to the
snooker halls or the bowling alleys, I would go back to do extra
work on my own.'

Such an attitude has blossomed in more recent times. An
increasingly professional outlook, both on and off the pitch, has
developed through enlightened coaches and players. They return
to the training pitch in the afternoon to practise technical aspects,
consider their diet very carefully, and seek to maintain their
physical and psychological preparedness through all aspects of
their daily living. Kenny Dalglish was an early example of professionalism. As described by Sean Fallon, his coach at Celtic,
Dalglish 'always looked after himself: no drinking, no smoking,
always early to bed, and trained hard'.

It may seem that a player nowadays cannot take the money
without taking the rest of the deal that accompanies it. Fans who
invest their money have a right to see their stars act professionally.
Unprofessional lifestyles can be equated with excess, as Emmanuel Petit put it: 'Too much alcohol kills the body, too much cocaine
kills the body, too much love kills the body. In fact too much of
anything kills the body. That's why too much football will kill the
game.'

As always tongue in cheek, Barry Fry suggested, 'Players have got a bigger responsibility than they realise. They have got to discipline themselves ... they should only drink, gamble and womanise in moderation.'

Before Glenn Hoddle's departure from the England job, one of his final acts was to offer Paul Gascoigne a lifeline, couched mostly in terms of lifestyle improvement. He said: 'Gazza's England career is not finished under me. But there are five things he needs to do: stop drinking, get fitter than ever before, change his diet, learn to control his emotions, and stay injury free.'

So what are the temptations, the alluring lifestyles, that threaten a player's footballing psyche and ultimately his career?

Alcohol

A swift half after training, a grape supper occasionally and a glass of the giggle water at some celebrity function seem all within limits. Excess, however, leads to top-heavy, wobbly-legged inebriation. When the amber nectar begins to dominate, influence a lifestyle and affect the way a player construes himself, he is in trouble. A few notable examples:

A drink never did any harm

'Andy Goram – the man with the safest hands in football, especially when there happens to be a white wine and soda clasped in them.' (Ally McCoist, on the Rangers goalie)

'I walked into the Celtic directors' lounge with my Rangers strip on. I went to the bar and had a double whisky ten minutes before the game.' (Paul Gascoigne, explaining his pre-match behaviour before his first Old Firm derby)

'There are one or two players about who'd like the competition renamed the Vodka & Coca-Cola Cup.' (Ron Atkinson)

Frank McAvennie: 'I don't think anything really affected him. All he seemed worried about was going out and drinking.' (Julian Dicks)

Indeed, it is something to be admired

'My hero's Bryan Robson. He's the only player I've ever known who could drink 16 pints and still play football the next day.' (Paul Gascoigne, eulogising over a man he later signed for at Middlesbrough)

'Our fans like people like Keith Gillespie – they relate to people who like to have a drink and get into trouble.' (Douglas Hall, Newcastle United chairman)

The repercussions

'On last season's pre-season tour, my room-mate returned blind drunk. Mistaking my bed for the toilet, he relieved himself all over it with me inside.' (Pat Nevin, keeping mum on the voiding culprit, during his stint at Tranmere Rovers)

'When I woke up the next morning, my bed was soaked and a chambermaid was standing in the room holding her nose and saying "pee pee".' (Tony Adams, in West Germany with England for the 1988 European Championships)

'Don Shanks and Stan Bowles spent the night in a Belgian jail after a sozzled Shanks had alarmed guests at a restaurant by crawling over the floor as if in the throes of an epileptic fit.' (Rob Steen)

A dawning realisation that we have a problem

'We quickly realised he [Paul Gascoigne] liked a drink – certainly a lot more than the other players.' (Zdenek Zeman, Roma)

'Gascoigne's a fantastic player when he isn't drunk.' (Brian Laudrup at Rangers)

'He [George Graham] would make the odd remark like "You're coming in a bit drunk, Tony. Watch that."' (Tony Adams)

Denial

'On a boys' night out after the game, the most I'll have is
seven or eight pints of lager. That, to me, isn't being drunk.'
(Charlie Nicholas)

'All the great players I've known enjoyed a good drink.' (Jim
Baxter)

'I like a drink and I like a party, but I'll be flat out in training
the next day, even if it's my day off.' (Carlton Palmer)

'People say I've squandered a fortune on birds and booze,
but as my old mate Stan Bowles said, it's better than
wasting it.' (Frank Worthington)

'Our players don't bloody drink for a start. There are no 12
pints a night men here.' (Bobby Robson at Porto)

Rationalisation:

'It is usually the legendary drinkers at a club who are the best
trainers. Okay, they go out and get into an unathletic state
but, come the next training day, they put in more effort
than the non-drinkers because they feel they have to.' (John
Colquhoun, Hearts. Unathletic being the operative word)

'Paul [Gascoigne] likes a few pints now and again, and I'm
sure he will give me a little bit of grief from time to time, but
it will be worth it. I'm sure he'll keep the spirits high, on the
pitch.' (Bryan Robson, signing the wayward one for
Middlesbrough, with a neat turn of phrase)

'You drink to celebrate a victory, and I had more to celebrate
than most.' (Brian Clough, rationalising his behaviour)

Self-disclosure

'I can drink like a chimney.' (Duncan Ferguson, using an
interesting metaphor)

'The legs aren't doing too bad and the lungs are okay. The
liver is rotted and will probably be finished off if we get the
right result on Sunday.' (Stuart McCall of Bradford City,

prior to a crunch match at Wolves, where victory would see them promoted to the Premiership)

Better the dire drink than the boredom of life

'Booze acted for me as an anaesthetic to avoid intense feelings, bad or good.' (Tony Adams)
'What's so great about reality? My reality stank. I was ready for a bender.' (Tony Adams, the day after England bowed out of Euro '96)

The low ebb

'I was the winner who had lost when it came to alcohol.' (Tony Adams, explaining his descent into alcoholism)
'I was going through the shakes and all the shit that accompanies the death rattle of active alcoholism.' (Tony Adams)

The professional approach

'If you come in smelling of drink on a Thursday, you're not playing on a Saturday. I'll not fine you, but I'll say, "You can explain it to the press why you're not playing, explain to the fans, these people who give you all that money, how you've been disrespectful to the people you play with."' (Gordon Strachan of Coventry City)

Gambling

The Stan Bowles way:

'If Stan Bowles could pass a betting shop the way he passes the ball he'd be a rich man.' (Ernie Tagg, his manager at Crewe Alexandra)
'It's reported that Stan Bowles endeavoured to discover the result of the 3.15 or the 4.20 by asking people in the stands, during the match.' (Rob Steen)

'To Stan Bowles, football was merely a means of sustaining an abiding passion for gambling, for having a stake in the uncertain, for walking a tightrope.' (Rob Steen)

'Stan Bowles' weakness was off the field, where he was a compulsive gambler.' (Terry Venables)

According to Rob Steen in *The Mavericks*, the most Stan Bowles won in a day was '£18,000, the biggest loss being £15,000'. Bowles took his obsession to some lengths. When playing for Carlisle United, he once came off the pitch depressed, 'having bet a colleague he could nutmeg the Spurs right back 20 times during the course of the game, and [he] had managed only 16'.

There are other punters who dally with the wage packet:

'The only advice I ever had about money was from turf accountants.' (Jim Baxter)

'I went training once with £4,500 in my pocket and ran out of petrol on the way home because I'd spent the lot [betting on the horses]. I had to hitch a lift.' (Steve Claridge)

'I've gambled a lot – horses, dogs, you name it, I've probably done it. I wish I'd never gambled.' (Charlie George)

Duncan Ferguson: 'He should stick to looking after pigeons and avoid the bookies.' (Jim Baxter)

'The only treble we normally get involved in is a bet on the horses or dogs.' (Robbie Earle, Wimbledon)

'They can't gamble here because they don't get any money.' (Joe Kinnear, denying any gambling with the crazy gang)

Perhaps things are changing, however:

'When I first came here we used to have the racing on the telly in the dressing room until five to three. Now everyone's stretching and preparing mentally for the game.' (Erland Johnsen)

'I've got a choice to make – either I go back to the booze and the gambling or I go the other way.' (Paul Merson)

Diet

The British way:

> 'The players eat sausages, fried eggs and beans before a
> game. After an away trip the club will lay on beers for the
> coach trip home.' (Lionel Perez, Sunderland keeper,
> learning the native ways)
> 'We won't change. Okay, maybe peas with the fish and chips
> from now on.' (John Hendrie, as Barnsley reach the
> Premiership)
> 'Two months ago I changed the players' pre-match meal to
> two meat and potato pies. That day we beat Huddersfield
> so I kept the order with our catering manager.' (Gary
> Megson, Stockport County)
> 'The food in Scotland is similar to Germany – McDonald's
> burgers.' (Jorg Albertz, Rangers)
> 'Tony Currie used to get on the coach with a pocket full of
> chocolate caramels and wolf them down like a compulsive
> eater.' (Ken Furphy, his manager at Sheffield United)
> 'Fruit is very good for you. I particularly like Terry's
> Chocolate Oranges.' (Paul Gascoigne)
> 'I've been on that peach diet. I eat everything but peaches.'
> (Paul Gascoigne again)

In step the dieticians:

> 'Food is an important part of a balanced diet.'
> (Fran Lebowitz)
> 'Diet is one jigsaw in the whole map.' (Everton dietician)

Perhaps a change is occurring:

> 'It's funny looking back, but I used to meet Vinnie Jones
> down the cafe, have sausage, egg, bacon, beans and a fried
> slice and then go off to training. Now it's all pasta, rice and
> lots of vegetables.' (Dennis Wise)

'We used to go away on Friday nights and Lou Macari
   wouldn't let us have chips or dessert.' (A miffed Julian
   Dicks, reflecting on his new manager)
'I still eat bananas. And seaweed. I may not be a
   better player, but I'm a better swimmer.' (Gordon
   Strachan)
'When you go abroad you can't be Johnny Foreigner. You've
   got to be one of them. If they're eating funny things on
   plates, then you eat funny things on plates.' (Steve
   Archibald at Barcelona)
'I would never eat haggis, not if you paid me.' (Marc Rieper,
   taking an alternative view by objecting to the local culture
   as he signs for Celtic)
'Players are a lot more professional in their attitudes now
   and it's rare to see someone come back from the summer
   two or three stone overweight.' (Gareth Southgate)

Drugs

Dalliance with eastern substances may lead to insidious ruination.
A 1991 random dope test on Diego Maradona came out positive
for cocaine. In 1994 the same player was tested positive for a
cocktail of five banned ephedrine-based substances at the World
Cup. 'I took those pills as if they were aspirin,' he said. He was
summarily kicked out of the tournament. Chris Armstrong was
out of football for two weeks after tests showed traces of
cannabis. In 1996 Fabien Barthez, the French goalkeeper, who
went on to win the World Cup in 1998, was banned for two
months after tests showed traces of cannabis.

'Cocaine is the footballer's drug. It's expensive and
   glamorous with that champagne image.' (Mark Dennis)
'I wasn't addicted to coke. I was addicted to the lifestyle.'
   (Frank McAvennie)
'Paul Merson's done so much work for the lesser known, but
   equally important white nose day.' (Hugh Grant, reflecting
   on Red Nose Day)

The nightlife

Lee Sharpe was barred from a night-club after a 'mystery incident'. George Best was banned from Tramps for fighting, which included some fists in a bust up with Michael Caine. Faustino Asprilla's club house was smashed up after a party. Jamie Caragher, dressed as the Hunchback of Notre Dame at the Liverpool Christmas party, allegedly performed explicit sex acts with a stripper.

'There was the stuff I managed to keep private: running up a bill for £5,800 in a night-club springs to mind; smashing bottles over my head as a party piece.' (Tony Adams)

'I realise it may have looked bad.' (Teddy Sheringham, making a compendious apology after being photographed at dawn in a Portuguese night-club days before the dawn of the 1998 World Cup)

'In my private life, I do what I like, and whoever doesn't like it can get stuffed. The night is my friend. If I don't go out, I don't score.' (Romario, with an interesting turn of phrase)

'I never went to Stringfellows that much. I preferred Tramps.' (Charlie Nicholas)

'It's not the sex that tires out young players, it's staying up all night looking for it.' (Clemens Westerhof, Nigeria's Dutch coach)

'Sometimes you need a release from football and Gazza's way is to have a couple of drinks with celebrities and high profile friends … Gazza likes to drink with his mates and have a bit of daft banter.' (Bryan Robson)

'Shall we say, in football parlance, he isn't over the moon.' (Detective Chief Inspector John Davis, on arresting Roy Keane for an alleged assault on two women in a Manchester night-club)

And then in steps the level-headed one:

'I tend to buy family men. With a married player you generally know he is at home in the evening, watching Coronation Street.' (Bruce Rioch)

Cars

'Apart from a flutter, good food, music and, of course, wine and women, my other consuming passion in life – if you don't count football – is cars,' announced Frank Worthington, embracing most of life's vices. Kevin Campbell has been fined and banned for a driving offence. Tony Adams served four months in jail after his car hit a wall at the end of a pitch-length skid whilst he was over the limit. Paul Merson was fined and banned after his swanky new motor ricocheted off a lamppost and into two other vehicles. Jan Molby was jailed for three months for serious driving offences, including a car chase with police at 100 mph on the wrong side of the road. Enough, enough …

Women

Footballers are little different from the red-blooded fans who go to watch them. But, as celebrities, their dalliance with the fairer sex makes better news and pictures. After all, who is interested in a pimply Pompey supporter's exploits with the local totty? George Best, who in contrast is newsworthy, boasts as one of his 'conquests' Georgie Lawton, the daughter of Ruth Ellis, the last woman to be executed in Britain. The insights of a few others:

'It's very difficult to go out. All the women want to bed me.'
(David Ginola, in typical confident manner)
'My chat-up line used to be, "I know a lot of Page Three birds, so I know a lot about boobs – show me your boobs and I'll see how they compare."' (Frank McAvennie, with a tad less of the Gallic charm)
'After a game Italian footballers like to relax with a few glasses of wine. Scottish players prefer to go looking for a bevvy and a shag.' (Jim Duffy, manager of Hibs, consolidating a view of the soccer star north of the border)

'I'm here to earn big money at Tottenham and to meet English girls.' (Moussa Saib)

'Drink wasn't the problem with George [Best] in the beginning. It was the girls. But finding the girls took him to places where he drank.' (Terry Venables)

Views from the other side:

Ryan Giggs: 'He's been playing crap since he met me.' (Dani Behr, when she was his girlfriend)

'Footballers are only interested in drinking, clothes and the size of their willies.' (Karen Brady, Birmingham City's managing director)

'I would have felt better about it if she'd been a nice, attractive woman. But our Rottweiler, Maggie, is more attractive than she is.' (Sam Holdsworth, Dean's wife, on his exploits away from home)

The debate over sex as an energiser or distraction rages on:

'Of course a player can have sexual intercourse before a match and play a blinder. But if he did it for six months he'd be a decrepit old man. It takes strength away from the body.' (Bill Shankly)

'Sex is one of the most relaxing things you can do, so the players should do it whenever they feel like it … as long as you don't do it during a game.' (Eric Hall)

'[Dave] Sexton once went through a phase of telling players not to make love the night before a game. On a Saturday morning Ossie [Peter Osgood] would promise him that he hadn't made love the previous night, omitting to mention the fact that he'd got his leg over with an air hostess that morning.' (Ian Hutchinson)

And then the true professional:

'I never squeezed spots on my face because I wanted to be

repulsive and keep girls away.' (Alan Ball. Dedication, or what?)

'I'm finding it difficult to find a girlfriend in Barnsley, or to settle into a decent way of life. The girls are far uglier than the ones back in Belgrade or Skopje and drink too much beer.' (Georgi Hristov. Mad, or what?)

The thin blue line

Inevitably a scrape with the law enforcement agencies makes good press, but the variety of offences may come as a surprise. Those sentenced include:

Fined

- Ray Parlour, for assaulting a taxi driver in Hong Kong.
- Lee Bowyer, for affray after hurling chairs at McDonald's staff.
- Ivan Petrov, of Bulgaria, for shoplifting two pairs of trousers on the eve of a European Championship qualifying game with Wales.
- Peter Storey, for not stopping at a crossing and head-butting a lollipop man.
- Duncan Ferguson, for a breach of the peace and assault after head-butting a policeman.
- Duncan Ferguson, for punching a postman on crutches.
- Noel Whelan, for attacking a shop front with his foot.

Payment of damages

- Charlie Nicholas ordered to pay £1,300 to a girl for assault after the claimant argued with Nicholas for stealing one of her chips

Community service

- Eric Cantona, 120 hours, for common assault in his kung-fu style kick on a fan at Selhurst Park.

- Vinnie Jones, 100 hours, for assaulting a neighbour.

Probation
- Duncan Ferguson, 12 months, for assault on a stranger in a pub, knocking him off a bar stool.

Suspended jail sentence

- Peter Storey, 6 months, for attacking a traffic warden.
- Peter Storey, 12 months, for running a brothel.
- Faustino Asprilla, for possession of a firearm after an incident in a crowded bar.

Prison sentence, overturned on appeal
- Dennis Wise, for assaulting a 65-year-old taxi driver.

A stretch
- Peter Storey, 4 weeks, for smuggling pornographic videos into England in the spare tyre of his car.
- Mickey Thomas, 18 months, for passing forged notes to YTS players.
- Duncan Ferguson, the 'Birdman of Barlinnie', 3 months, for assaulting Raith Rovers full back, John McStay.
- Rene Higuita (of scorpion kick fame) in Colombia, for his part in the 'release' of a kidnapped girl from one of the drug gangs.
- Jamie Lawrence, 26 months, for armed robbery.
- Peter Storey, for his involvement in financing a scheme to counterfeit gold half sovereigns.
- Graham Rix, after pleading guilty to sexual offences against an under-age girl.
- James Kelly of Wolverhampton Wanderers, 5 years, for kicking a hotel porter to death.

Gone missing

Occasionally a player finds his lifestyle ever so slightly affects a willingness to turn up for training. But then we all feel a tad reluctant to turn in once in a while. Some noted absentees:

'Alan Hudson would never turn up on a Monday morning training. Headache, flu, everything but having a baby.' (Dave Webb)

'It's always in the back of my mind that Paul [McGrath] might have more problems with his knees, or that he might not bloody turn up for the World Cup.' (Jack Charlton)

Eric Cantona: 'When he couldn't have his own way he just took his bat home ... he went missing, back to his music, painting and poetry.' (Howard Wilkinson)

'Radiciou went missing on the way to the Stockport game because he thought he was going to be sub.' (Harry Redknapp)

'We got a fax from Bogotá saying Asprilla was stranded there because the plane couldn't go. But the plane did go, and he wasn't on it. We don't know where he is.' (Kevin Keegan)

'If Emerson does not play for us, he can sit on the beach in Brazil or on the quayside in Barcelona watching the ships sail by.' (Steve Gibson of Middlesbrough, in Otis Redding mood)

'George Best took liberties by just not bothering to turn up if he'd had a heavy night. He was not only abusing himself but abusing other people's respect for him.' (Bobby Moore)

'I've always had a reputation for going missing – Miss England, Miss United Kingdom, Miss World ...' (George Best)

Gordon Strachan, a paragon of professionalism himself, points to his Coventry City captain as a shining example of how the modern player might conduct himself. He said, 'Just walking about the training ground Gary McAllister's a great example, a guideline to how my players should behave on and off the pitch. I've got another two here like that, Nilsson and Steve Ogrizovic, perfect examples of the way you should train, the way you should eat and the way to behave.' That says it all really.

Sources

Atkinson, R. (1998) *Big Ron: A Different Ball Game*. London, André Deutsch.

Ball, P. and Shaw, P. (1991) *Football Quotations*. London, Stanley Paul.

Ball, P. and Shaw, P. (1996) *The Umbro Book of Football Quotations*. London, Ebury Press.

Best, G. (1990) *The Good, the Bad and the Bubbly*. London, Pan.

Blows, K. (1996) *Terminator: The Authorised Julian Dicks Story*. Leicester, Polar.

Bowler, D. (1996) *Shanks: The Authorised Biography of Bill Shankly*. London, Orion.

Butler, R. And Galvin, P. (1999) *Golf: A Mind Game*. Cookham, Queensgate.

Charlton, J. (1996) *Jack Charlton: The Autobiography*. London, Partridge Press.

Cowan, T. (1998) *On the Edge*. Huddersfield, Castlegate Mill.

Four Four Two.

Freddi, C. (1996) *The Guinness Book of Football Blunders*. London, Guinness.

Gekoski, R. (1998) *Staying Up*. London, Little, Brown.

Gray, A. (1999) *Flat Back Four*. London, Boxtree.

Harris, H. (1997) *Ruud Gullit: Portrait of a Genius*. London, Collins Willow.

Hill, D. (1989) *Out of His Skin*. London, Faber & Faber.

Hutchinson, R. (1995) *It Is Now*. Edinburgh, Mainstream.

James, S. (1990) *Sporting Quotations*. Edinburgh, Chambers.

Jarman, C. (1990) *The Guinness Dictionary of Sports Quotations*. Enfield, Guinness.

Jarman, C. (1996) *The Guinness Book of Humorous Sports Quotations*. Enfield, Guinness.

Kelly, S.F. (1997) *Dalglish*. London, Headline.

Lambert, C. (1997) *The Boss*. London, Vista.

MacDonald, K. (1999) *Scottish Football Quotations*. Edinburgh, Mainstream.

Pelé and Fish, R.L. (1977) *Pelé: My Life and the Beautiful Game*. London, New English Library.

Powell, J. (1993) *Bobby Moore: The Life and Times of a Sporting Hero*. London, Robson Books.

Reynolds, M. (1996) *The Wrong Kind of Shirts*. London, Fourth Estate.

Reynolds, M. (1997) *The Wrong Kind of Shirts 2*. London, Fourth Estate.

Reynolds, M. (1998) *The Wrong Kind of Shirts '98*. London, Fourth Estate.

Simpson, P. and Spiller, R. (1997) *Football Intelligence*. London, Pan.

Steen, R. (1997) *The Mavericks*. Edinburgh, Mainstream.

Thompson, P. (1996) *Do That Again Son and I'll Break Your Legs*. London, Virgin.

Tibballs, G. (1999) *Do I Not Like That?* London, Virgin.

Williams, R. (1996) *Football Babylon*. London, Virgin.

Worthington, F. (1994) *One Hump or Two?* Leicester, ACL & Polar.

Q

Other books from Queensgate Publications

Golf: A Mind Game
Richard Butler and Peter Galvin

Professional psychologists – and amateur golfers – Richard Butler and Peter Galvin have written this book as a layman's guide to the complex world of golf psychology and the role it can play in order to improve our game.

Distinctly off-beat in approach, and with a collection of hilarious cartoons by illustrator Geo Parkin, *Golf: A Mind Game* is a technical manual for the mind, designed for the golf course, with a resonance that carries far beyond the 18th hole

GOLF — A Mind Game

Richard Butler and Peter Galvin
with illustrations by Geo Parkin

1-902655-03-6

Q

Motor sport books from Queensgate Publications

Track Record Maurice Rowe 1-902655-00-1

The photography of *The Motor* magazine's former Chief Photographer, Maurice Rowe. Over 300 black and white and colour images from F1 and sports cars, 1950-1980.

Racers 1948-1968 Doug Nye 1-902655-01-X

Part One of two volumes celebrating the greatest drivers in F1. Doug Nye selects his Top 20, from Wimille to Hulme. Lavishly illustrated with over 250 photographs.

Racers 1969-2000 Alan Henry 1-902655-028

Part Two of the *Racers* series, celebrating the modern era of Grand Prix. *Autocar*'s long-time correspondent profiles his star drivers from Jochen Rindt to Mika Häkkinen.

Schumi Alan Henry 1-902655-27-3

Alan Henry profiles the world's leading racing driver and examines his Grand Prix career to date, including his controversial return from 'that' Silverstone accident.

Mika   Alan Henry   1-902655-26-5

Biography of the likeable Finnish driver who recovered from a horrific practice accident at the end of the 1995 season to win back-to-back world titles for McLaren–Mercedes.

The Grand Prix Bible   Mike Lawrence   1-902655-25-7

Encyclopaedic facts and figures guide to Formula 1. Driver histories, race facts, circuit details, technical information: this is the ultimate armchair guide.

Also from Queensgate Publications

Action Guide Europe   Watkins/Grogan   1-902655-06-0

Queensgate is distributed in the UK by

MDL Sales
Macmillan Distribution Ltd
Brunel Road
Houndmills
Basingstoke
Hants RG21 6XS

Tel 01256 302775
Fax 01256 351437

Queensgate is distributed in the USA by

Trafalgar Square Publishing
PO Box 257
Howe Hill Road
North Pomfret
Vermont 05053

Tel 802 457 1911
Fax 802 457 1913
www.trafalgarsquarebooks.com